POLITY AND THEATRE IN HISTORICAL PERSPECTIVE

POLITY AND THEATER

IN HISTORICAL PERSPECTIVE

KAREN HERMASSI

UNIVERSITY OF CALIFORNIA PRESS

BERKELEY / LOS ANGELES / LONDON

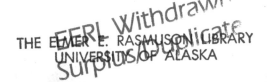

University of California Press
Berkeley and Los Angeles, California
University of California Press, Ltd.
London, England
Copyright © 1977 by
The Regents of the University of California
ISBN 0-520-03294-2
Library of Congress Catalog Card Number: 76-19971
Printed in the United States of America

1 2 3 4 5 6 7 8 9

I dedicate this book to
my parents,
my grandfather, Samuel;
and to my sister, Bette.

Contents

Preface

In recent decades, it has become increasingly fashionable to study politics and drama analogously. Although it belabors the obvious to announce that political essays are now permeated with the language of theatre—with "actors," "roles," "stages," "scenarios," and "audiences"—there is something both new and old in this analogy. Old, because polities have always affirmed power through symbols and expressed it through dramatic analogy. But new, in that we are no longer certain where the drama begins and the reality of state ends. The subtle lines between political performance as art and political performance as power have continually blurred.

In an effort to get at the differences and similarities between drama and politics, outstanding contemporary social scientists (Erving Goffman, Georges Gurvitch, Jean Duvignaud, and Elizabeth Burns, to mention a few) have undertaken to compare notions of action and structure in drama with their counterpart in society. But there has been little if any examination of theatre's actual meaning as an art form in relation to the questions of political and social significance. In this study, I will try to ground interpretations of politics and drama by returning to three historical periods of drama—Greek, Elizabethan, and contemporary—and exploring each as it evolved in relation to certain areas in the history of political thought.

It is the meaning and history of political thought that most concerns me here, and I have turned to this comparative study of dramatic art and politics not simply out of interdisciplinary interest but because, as I suggested above, I believe it is generic to the study of political theory itself. Judith Shklar best phrased this idea when she wrote in memory of the late Hannah Arendt, "Political philosophy is tragic thought. Without a dramatic sense of fate and mutability no rational intelligence would turn to this hideous subject."

In this work, I will be turning to political theory and dramatic art in order to concentrate on a theme that has always been common to both: that of public life. My sense of this theme has been affected, as for us all, by the atmosphere of disintegrating public confidence in America during the protracted Vietnam War and the subsequent experience of Watergate. This has been a time of painful reassessments of ourselves as a nation, and also, as T. S. Eliot wrote after the Second World War, a time when the very concepts that once endowed our political life with purpose are bereft of meaning—concepts like the public, the community, the state, and the culture. With these problems in mind, I have not intended to provide an exhaustive treatment of the world's theatres and their political settings but rather to explore certain relations between theatre and politics which enlarge and refine our understanding of what "political" means in our own time.

The special relationships between drama and politics are not duplicated anywhere else in the polity, and that is one of the reasons it is vital to try to sort them out. Another reason is that various theatres have served to document changes and developments of their political cultures to which we might never gain access but for their records of reenacted time and space. The specific historical crossroads we will attempt to traverse here are those of Aeschylus and the new city-state; Shakespeare and the newly emerging nation-state; and Brecht and the twentieth-century totalitarian state. Other theatres, particularly from Asia, enter the discussion not to season what is already a curried full course meal, but to suggest that the real gifts of drama worldwide may lie in its relationships to political order, which cut across the cultural fiction of east and west. In general, if we wish to make some headway at all in reconstructing the more significant crossroads of drama, politics, and history, and thereby gain insight into some of history's most memorable publics, we require far greater sensitivities to the tensions *within* the same society and an openness to the diverse cultural universes in which societies can express themselves.

The specific periods of drama and polity that will be the focus of this book were selected because they seem to constitute the more crucial turning points in the histories of both dramatic art and political order. For this purpose, the selection of plays has often been more restricted than my own preferences or those of the reader might dictate. In a study of this kind, the sin of omission seems almost inevitable; the materials are too rich and the space too limited. The theoretical focus must take precedence over specific plays because the theatres we esteem most highly tend to be related to the most significant developments in the history of the polity. Is it only coincidence that just as each decisive political foundation made its historical appearance (city, nation, democratic and communist revolutions, the bureaucratic-corporate state) it has been accompanied by the brief flourishing of remarkable drama? May it not be that the great theatres have detected their calling in each distinct political foundation and emerged to interpret the beginnings for us, not just as beginnings of a city or a nation, but as symbols of a tragic human vocation—to be forced, in desperation, to begin again? From the earliest cave paintings, it is apparent that men have always needed to see themselves as depicting their own collective lives. That they must also see themselves as eternal beginners may be the drama's best preserved text. Like Rilke's searching admonition, the drama has always told us, "Resolve to be always beginning."

A word about the organization of this book and the association between political theorist and dramatist in each Part. In one sense, the reader will find three separate historical and comparative essays on theatre and political order. Each relationship between dramatist and theorist is unique. In Part I, Aeschylus and Plato are discussed in a re-examination of tragedy and philosophy, which in their Greek context both center on a critique of the polis. The implications of Aeschylean drama for Platonic philosophy are reviewed. In Part II, Shakespeare and Saint Augustine are approached from a very different perspective. Here, I develop an interpretation of Shakespeare's tragic vision in terms of Augustine's theory of the City of God and the City of Man. I do not assume that Shakespeare read Augustine or self-consciously wrote drama in light of Augustine's theories, but rather suggest that the incommensurable despair of Shakespearian theatre and its particular drama-tization of polity may be more accessible to us in the frame-work of such a comparison. Part III proceeds with the first clear instance of a dramatist acknowledging the vital in-fluence of a political theory, the theory of Karl Marx, upon his vision. But by the time we get to Brecht, the historical context of political order (public, city, and state) is being decimated in twentieth-century struggles for world power, and a new question appears in the study of polity and theatre: have both dramatic and political forms lost their constituencies? What does the waning of theatre arts in our own time portend for the future of a national public life?

Yet, in another sense, the various Parts of this book are not distinct essays but historical reinterpretations of the

same theoretical approach to theatre that embraces politics, memory, and art throughout. This work at best only
touches the surface of a very complex matter, given how
relatively little we know about the phenomenon of memory
and politics in relation to art. Whether one speaks of the
political actor or the dramatic actor, the person will always
be, in the words of Rollo May, "that curious being who is
afflicted with memory. If he cannot integrate his memories into his self-image, he must pay for his failure by
neurosis or psychosis; and he tries, generally in vain, to
shake himself loose from the tormenting memories." The
identifying passion of the theatre throughout its distinguished history has been, thus, to rescue lost connections from an all-consuming present. I hope the reader will
find that the connections between theatre and political
traditions explored here will tend to outweigh in significance the more superficial contrasts between the different historical eras and are worthy of this return, from
cultural deserts in our own time, to a memorable and
complex past.

Acknowledgments

It has been my privilege to study with outstandingly talented teachers and to have had the support of colleagues, students and friends throughout the writing of this book.

I wish to mention with gratitude that I spent the year 1973–1974 as a Visiting Fellow at the Institute for Advanced Study at Princeton. With the excellent facilities and libraries of the Institute, I was able to completely redraft and compose much of this manuscript. I wish to thank in particular Dr. Carl Kaysen, Director, and Professor Clifford Geertz for their personal kindness and encouragement and the other Members that year for the many discussions from which I derived so much.

To Sheldon S. Wolin, I owe the very conception of this work as well as a studied reexamination of its conclusions. While he must not bear the blame for the latter, my debt to him as theorist, teacher, and friend continues. His several readings of the manuscript at different stages of completion have contributed to whatever real insight may emanate from it. Those of us who had the rare experience of studying with Professor Wolin during his years at the University of California at Berkeley will always regard that time as one in which the discipline of political theory, rather than removing us further from the world, enabled us to act more fully within it, to make painful political commitments in an increasingly difficult political universe. This book is somehow related to those years, and I cannot adequately express my own deep respect or the high regard in which his many students continue to hold him.

Hanna Pitkin and Robert N. Bellah also gave this manuscript considerable attention from its earliest stages. Hanna's incisive criticism helped me to integrate the disparate elements of the book's theoretical development and to press harder for a clarity of ideas that was often lacking. Robert Bellah, through his fine perception of both classical and contemporary social thought, was able to caution me against the less fruitful generalizations and to indicate the more significant directions for rewriting. I wish to thank both Professor Bellah and his wife, Melanie for their generous personal support and friendship during a troubled time when I was completing this study.

To Alain Renoir, I wish to express my deepest appreciation and affection, both for his professional devotion to classical studies which inspired my own research, and for his humor, which has been as essential as his friendship— without it one can hardly bear the world, and with it the world is not what matters most.

I wish to thank my splendid former colleagues at the Collegiate Seminar Program at the University of California, Berkeley: Charles Sellers, Charles Muscatine, Peter Dale Scott, Carolyn Iltis, Paul Plouffe, Gloria Bowles, Judith Van Allen, and my many fine students for their gracious and patient support of my research explorations during the last two years. In our seminars, I drew many ideas from the lively discussions and was able to recast my own thinking on some points that would have otherwise escaped my attention.

The manuscript was typed with care by Anna Marie Holt and Catharine Rhubart of the Institute for Advanced

Study at Princeton. And during the last month of work, I benefited from the special editorial assistance of Dr. Frederick Goldstein who contributed a more detached overall perspective to the book.

Finally, I wish to thank my friends Patricia Karlin Steinhour, Leah Shelleda, Dr. Darryl and Kayla Chagi, Leslie Schneider, Phyllis Killen, Deborah and Michael Rogin, Paul and Ruth Von Blum, and Anne and Raymond Poirier for the things one cannot exactly name but which make accomplishments like survival, the writing of books, and other impossible feats still possible.

K. H.
Berkeley

PART I. The Constructive Vision: Aeschylus and Plato

1. What Theatre Means

Relentless memory may lead to terror. Yet the very limits of our language and reality are exhausted by a memory that always fails. Between these two extremes of remembrance and forgetfulness, a peculiar new art form found its words and acts for the first time in recorded history, at the dawning of the fifth century B.C., in ancient Greece. This art of tragedy, as the theatre was first known, emerged in a tense and unprecedented coalescence of memory, vision, and language in the collective memory of a city, without which no theatre is possible. The first theatre in Athens was, then, as many scholars have asserted, rooted in the discovery of a mystery—but not the sort of mystery we have sometimes assumed. It was not a Dionysian rhapsody to expel fear, a feast after long fasting, but the mystery of recollection, recreated in the new art of drama.

Many contemporary cultures have experienced dread in collective memory, but it is a timeless condition, as the writings of Mircea Eliade have informed us. He perceives the collective memory as ahistorical; a process by which we have learned to elude the threatening presence of the world. Past events are never recorded as particular and irreversible in the immediate terrestrial context, but are transcended in a myth which translates all that is individual into an examplar.[1] Myth as effective harness on memory existed in many ancient cultures, and was capable of regenerating the human spirit by continual repetition of exemplars, or archetypes as Eliade calls them. Having accepted the "normality of suffering" in this life, the collective memory observed no inherent significance in the present acts of its community; these were "real" only insofar as they imitated or repeated an archetype.[2] Therefore, rich as this mythical reality was, and certain of its precedence over the world of the moment, it had no need for recreation in the theatre. Purging themselves of time's corrosions, these ancient communities desired "to have no 'memory,' not to record time, to content [themselves] with tolerating it simply as a dimension of [their] existence, but without 'interiorizing' it, without transforming it into consciousness."[3] These peoples had no need for an art of recollection, because no human experience was to be *passed on* through the generations, either of the self or the community, as memory to be reexamined and relived. Human experience was rather to be negated in myth, which was superior to the living event in their understanding.

This derogation of human action, history, and recollection bears greatly on the absence of theatres in Eliade's discussion, for the creation of drama presupposes, in its remote beginnings, what Northrop Frye has called the "language and myth of concern."[4] That is, it presupposes an entire community bound through its acts and assumptions to "other worlds, other beings, other lives, other dimensions of time and space."[5] The myth of concern develops traditionally within a preliterate, oral culture,

1. Mircea Eliade, *The Myth of the Eternal Return, or Cosmos and History*, R. Trask, trans., pp. 44ff.
2. *Ibid.*, p. 34.
3. *Ibid.*, p. 91.
4. Frye, "The Social Context of Literary Criticism," in *Sociology of Literature and Drama*, E. and T. Burns, eds., pp. 139-158.
5. *Ibid.*, p. 149.

completely dependent for survival on the fertile memory of its descendents. This was, of course, the sort of environment in which the Homeric epic thrived and in which theatre was eventually created—an environment of unwritten history and oral and ritual arts. In this environment, myth does not take the place of history; it rather assists the recollection of events so that some sort of historical picture of the culture is preserved through memory. The main point is that drama germinates only in this soil of collective memory, focused on its culture's past action with the view that learning from recollecting the past is an indispensable key to constructive action in the future. Recollection and action are thus wedded in the appearance of theatre, not merely because past action is being reordered and reconstructed in the art form but because to recollect and perceive the past are profoundly impassioned activities.[6]

The community of concern that matured into an audience for the Homeric epic awaited the right set of circumstances to become the audience of theatre. That unique set of circumstances was finally achieved when the transition of a relatively formless community of concern into a new public and city occurred in Greece between the seventh and fifth centuries B.C. Within this transition, the existence of a public was prior to the foundations of both city and theatre, and how the public began to take shape can best be seen in the specific distinctions between its new drama and the former epic. In his analysis of the epic and drama, George Lukacs gives us fundamentally two decisive differences, adapted in part from Hegel's theory of tragic action: first, drama emphasizes for the first time man as a social-moral being, whereas epic had focused upon the natural

---

6. The point that memory and perception are not passive is well treated by Edward T. Hall, *The Hidden Dimension*. Hall notes first that "perception depends upon memory or past stimulation, *i.e.* it has a *past* that lays the foundation for the perceptions of here and now" (p. 179). And perception itself is an active transaction "between man and his environment in which both participate" (p. 75).

world in which men were largely physical beings; and
second, the destiny of the individual in drama suddenly
becomes a symbol for the destiny of the entire community,
whereas in the epic an individual's destiny had been a mere
by-product of eternal conflicts between gods and nature.[7]
In this light, we can say that a two-fold conception of the
public also emerged as the epic began to give way to the
development of dramatic art: a public that began as a
community now regarding itself as a moral body, that is as a
body now taking responsibility for its own actions; and a
new political order—the city—in which the public would
structure and record its history and action. In terms of
these two new conceptions of public life, the theatre was
slowly created to assist the city's collective memory through
reenactment of individual and collective tragedy, whose
action would now be defined as *larger than life can bear*. This
contrasts clearly with the epic, in which the scale of action
was deliberately superhuman. The epic was not intended
to instruct young men in the art of community action as
much as to enthrall them in an extraordinary catastrophe
that was not completely of their own doing.

Thus far, we can say that the central conception of
memory as a "retelling" in the epic of pre-polis Greece
undergoes a subtle modification in the appearance of
theatre after the polis. For Aeschylus wished to *transform*,
not simply preserve, the collective memory of his city,
demanding for the first time that myth be burdened by the
raw edges of history. Where the populace, in Eliade's
analysis, was anesthetized against the vulnerability of historical persons and the immediacy of events through their

7. G. Lukacs, "Approximation to Life in the Novel and the Play," in *Sociology of Literature and Drama*, E. and T. Burns, eds., p. 284. Hegel wrote that the former single conflict of the epic becomes the active self-assertion of the individual in *collision* with a totality of circumstances and diverse ends, forming multiple conflicts in drama. Dramatic action rests essentially on this collision. See *Hegel on Tragedy*, A. and H. Paolucci, eds. (Doubleday Anchor, N.Y., 1962), pp. 12-15.

transfiguration in the myth, Aeschylean tragedy would underscore decision and risk by closing in on historical events and persons, act by act, heightening their proximity to ourselves like that of the audience to the actors. The event could not be abolished in dramatic portrayal; on the contrary, it is more starkly present. The mythical sense of time could still in this way be preserved: permanence rather than evolution, "cyclic time and eternal repetition" more than linear or "perpetual transformation."[8] However, this same sense of time was to confirm in theatre what in myth had been its contradiction: the compelling significance of historical sequence and human action.

Tragedy was above all not the imitation of an action, as Aristotle would later write, but the *interpretation* of action by reconstituting an event before a public audience of witnesses. For this public, the dramatic performance was either recollected from a host of forgotten memories of ancestors and cities or retained as a personal memory of some newly perceived event. It was, in any case, relived in the observance, for the Greek tragedians and their audiences believed that action was even more profoundly experienced by spectators to reenactment than by actors in the original act itself. This was true because drama was both act and symbol in the same moment. The revelations of this instant coexistence far exceeded those of action in daily life, which even when historically significant was too divorced from critical thought to be helpful in the future. It was good but not sufficient that action be memorable— it had also to be recollected in the reflective art of theatre.

Given this significance of recollection for drama, it is best at this juncture to explore with some care the differences in meaning between collective memory and recollection as they relate to the meaning of theatre. First, one must acknowledge the entire tradition of memory as an art that

8. Jacqueline de Romilly, *Time in Greek Tragedy*, pp. 24-25.

exists in European culture commencing with Plato and
Aristotle.[9] In this long and remarkable tradition, memory
has consistently been conceived of as both natural and
artificial. Natural memory is regarded as simply part of
thought itself, a faculty of birth and not training. To
Socrates, we owe the metaphor of wax that is imprinted by
experience and language: "we hold the wax under the
perceptions and conceptions and imprint them on it, as if
we were taking the impressions of signet rings."[10] Aristotle
enlarged on this in an important way by adding that
memory and imagination occupy the same part of the soul.
Thus natural memory is an accumulation of mental images
(scenes imagined) from the past, and the collective memory
comprises the mental images of a people's entire history.

The notion of artificial memory is a response, for Aristotle, to the fact that natural memory is not easily refreshed
and that its mental pictures are not enduring. Most minds
are frail in their powers of memory and must be assisted,
for example, by the actual staging of mental pictures as
moving portraits of the past to stir remembrance in the
present. Artificial memory, then, is the strengthening of an
individual's or community's memories through art, rendering the images more immediate and accessible to the
necessities of life in the present. Theatre, in this sense,
affords the city an artificial memory, a sort of memory bank
in which the past, as conjured up by the dramatist, is
deposited and our ability to draw from it is kept in a certain
balance. We must not recall too much too fast and like
Hamlet become incapacitated, nor remember too little and

9. See Frances Yates' excellent study, *The Art of Memory*.
10. Plato, *Theaetetus*, 191, tr. John McDowell. Contemporary versions of this
metaphor merely reflect technological change—the wax becomes a tape recorder
or video tape—without attending to the philosophical dilemma of memory as a
tabula rasa for sense impressions in the world. I believe Plato's theory of
recollection is, at least, more cognizant of the active qualities of mind in which the
changing meaning of memory can find its place, despite the wax metaphor.
Wittgenstein warns us of the latter in discussing the misleading concept of the
"inner picture," in *Philosophical Investigations*, II, xi, tr. G. E. M. Anscombe, p. 196e.

like the Zeus of *Prometheus Bound* repeat our errors to self-
destruction. The pictures of the past we witness on the
stage will be such that as we recall them, our motives and
judgments will be better informed in the present. For
instance, when Aeschylus put the Persian War before his
Athenian audience, he selected to portray it from the perspective of the invading enemy, so that the finest moment
of Athenian history would be remembered as another
people's defeat; for the lesson and memory of defeat was
far more significant, in Aeschylean drama, than ritual celebrations of victory, from which nothing could be retained
save vanity.

Recollection, on the other hand, is distinguished from
memory in that it constitutes "a deliberate effort to find
one's way among the contents of memory, hunting among
its contents for what one is trying to recollect."[11] Like Plato,
Aristotle perceives recollection as the recovery of knowledge from memory. Recollection is the art of finding what
we must know, defined as what we must "not forget."[12] In
Plato's theory of knowledge as recollection, we are to
assume that all we know is being remembered and not
introduced for the first time; our knowledge must then
precede our birth in this world and continue after the body
dies in the eternal migrations of the soul (psyche). The only
foundation for knowledge, therefore, is memory, which is
accessible only to those souls open to the recollection of life
in the past. Socrates tells us, however, that even when one is
at last resigned to the task of knowing as recollecting, one is
confronted by the problem that the mind is usually a poor
agent of memory, and that only certain psyches remember
well:

When the wax in someone's mind is thick, copious, smooth, and
worked to a proper consistency, then, when the things which
come through the senses are imprinted on that tablet of the heart,

11. Yates, *The Art of Memory*, p. 34.
12. *Theaetetus*, 191.

as Homer calls it, in an obscure allusion to its similarity to wax, the imprints which come into being in those people and under those conditions are clear, and adequately deep, and they last a long time. To begin with, people of that sort are good learners; secondly, they have good memories; and third, they don't transpose their imprints with respect to their perceptions, but make true judgments. Because, since their imprints are clear and well spaced, they are quick to allot each set of things to the imprints that belong to them . . . and those people are called wise.[13]

Socrates speaks of the psyche, whose memory functions well, as having specific properties in its wax that keep it from confusion. He is reiterating the theme that remembering, just as learning, demands training and exercise. Wax that is "thick, copious, smooth and worked to a proper consistency" will have been molded since childhood in the acuities of language, music, and mathematics. From the retention of figures and symbols, and the discipline of harmony, the maturing psyche will aspire to conceptual and dialectical thought. Continuing education will depend, at each stage, upon the psyche's capacity for recollection which must transcend the retention of *facts* and is described above as having imprints that are "clear, and adequately deep, and . . . last a long time . . . they don't transpose their imprints with respect to their perceptions, but make true judgments." The meanings of these qualifications for recollection are obviously far more complex than the mere imprint of a signet ring in wax.

It could be said that these qualifications are appropriate to a mind still conceived of as a container or, at best, a stationary camera which simply gathers in-focus snapshots of an empirical world that "forces" itself upon the viewer. However, neither of these two metaphors suffices in relation to "true judgments" and neither is adequate for a psyche that must allot each memory to an appropriate

13. *Theaetetus*, 194.

place with respect to the environment from which it comes.[14]

With the benefit of Freud's language and concepts, the contemporary analyst might infer the following from Socrates' description of the active recollecting psyche: that such a mind had awareness of its repressions in the unconscious; that it had begun to clear the path of memory, creating space for it by trying to remove the mental walls erected against memory either because of personal suffering or cultural intervention. Once the psyche is receptive to the sourceless wellsprings of memory, however, the awesome question remains: how to determine the significance of that which is recollected or stored for future reference? In other words, how does the psyche become its own best historian? The task of distributing memory in its proper place or allotting significance in recollection is of central concern in the Platonic dialogues, just as it was the primary objective of the first dramatists. Thus, Plato writes his philosophy in dialogue, as dramatic reenactments, not merely because he is selecting a familiar literary form but because his Socrates cannot reveal the nature of his pursuits in any other form. The Platonic dialogues are dramas of human memory in conflict. What is essential, from the perspective of this discussion, is not the particular Socratic argument being carried forward but the fact that Socrates

14. There is an element of time in the difference between these conceptions of memory that is crucial. The memory of an experience is not the same as its meaning. Memory is an image that comes to mind, so to speak, but its meaning may have nothing to do with this image being retained as such. A memory has rather been altered over time in the mind—which has, like theatre itself, reconstructed a picture of the past many times *from* memory. Wittgenstein's example of grief makes the point well: "My grief is no longer the same; a memory which was still unbearable to me a year ago is now no longer so. That is a result of observation. When do we say that any one is observing? Roughly: when he puts himself in a favorable position to receive certain impressions in order (for example) to describe what they tell him." We might want to call this a good description of recollecting. (*Philosophical Investigations*, II ix, p. 187e.)

cannot recall what he seeks to know in any other way except the dialogue.

The points of Platonic philosophy are made by a tragic hero always in collision with the suppositions and intentions of other antagonists, particularly of course the sophists. Take, for example, the problem of whether virtue can be taught. We discover that the answer to what can be taught is like the answer to what can be known. In the *Meno*, 93-95, Socrates lamentably concludes that virtue cannot be taught, because history has confirmed that virtue in the father cannot be passed on to his sons. Athenians renowned for their virtue, like Themistocles, Aristides, Pericles, and Thucydides, were all able to instruct their sons in horsemanship, music, and gymnastics, but they were not able to teach them virtue because their own virtue was not a function of their knowing the good, or their knowledge. It was, rather, a divine spirit (daimon) dwelling in them, enabling them to act upon "true opinion" which they acquire neither by nature nor instruction. For they do not discover knowledge of the good by knowing in advance what they are seeking; and yet precisely they do discover the good. *The Meno* asks us to define this *discovery*, and we come to understand it as recollection. They are discovering what they have already known before. For Plato, this dialogue is the turning point at which both politics and poetry are subject to the same fleeting inspirations without the benefit of true knowledge, until he attempts to establish political virtue through public education in the setting of the *Republic*.[15]

True opinion could be of some use in teaching virtue, politics being what it is, if actions based upon true opinion could be recollected by others in the same community and thus become, as it were, precedents for virtue. Socrates

15. The cost there, however, as Sheldon Wolin has shown, is that of the political material itself—vicissitude and conflict. *Politics and Vision*, pp. 28-68.

defines recollection, in this instance, as "fastening" true
opinion (that is, giving a living example of virtuous action)
in the human soul (*Meno*, 98). Unfortunately, however,
true opinion tends to be like the images of Daedalus,
"because they require to be fastened in order to keep them,
and if they are not fastened they will play truant and run
away" (*Meno*, 97). In other words, virtue cannot be taught,
because it is based on true opinion which is not fastened in
the mind's eye over time or remembered. We tend to forget
the experience or example of virtue, and since no groundwork of understanding underlies the action, the memory
of the act is *all* we have in relation to human virtue. There
are no teachers of virtue, because the experience of virtue
in one lifetime cannot be extended to the next through
memory without some particular assistance. In memory,
virtue must be entertained in all its complexities as well: is it
wrong to take another's life? asks Aeschylus; and the
Oresteia tells us "yes" in one tragedy, and "no" in the next.
Only an audience whose minds can move with, and tolerate, the differences in recollecting the two acts of murder
can possibly learn from the answers.

But no sooner is this declared than the paradox of
Socrates' position, as a teacher and a teacher devoted to the
study of virtue and wisdom, consumes the beleaguered
reader. Why has Plato submitted us to this vain search for
something that cannot be learned? Is it that the search for
justice itself, in the context of Plato's dialogues, must
become part of our living experience as he dramatizes it for
us? We see the ways in which this search is not readily available to us in the absence of virtue as a *living act*. Here, a
small ray of light begins to illuminate theatre's purpose as
recollection. For because most aspects of human culture
can be taught and transmitted—religion, science, art, craft,
language—they can be retained in memory given the
context of the polis or an on-going political culture, even

though they are not in some senses part of one's particular life experience. Obviously, one can understand and appreciate the powers and beauties of style in music and sculpture without being able to create a work of art oneself. But, Plato would tell us, one cannot value the excellence of virtue without the memory of its acts, and how do we preserve human acts in the same way beauty and style are preserved in music and sculpture? The chained cave-dweller would rather kill than be brought out into the light, for the light is completely foreign to his recollection. The tragic aspect of virtue is that it dies, unlike a work of art, with each generation, unless it can somehow be reenacted and witnessed once again.

This is the reason Plato's philosophy comes to center on the polis (the *Republic*), in which an individual's experience within a public will be structured in such a way that it will be remembered across generations, and virtue will be learned in a city that does not change from one generation to the next. The point here is that Plato's *Republic* becomes a permanent "memory place" in which the task of recollection can be fully accomplished by the rulers.[16] Perhaps this is why there is no place for drama in the *Republic*; the dramatic vocation of memory has been incorporated into the political.

But the actual polis of Athens, as we know, did not evade the devastations of flux and current; on the contrary, few societies given their technological capacities have undergone so much change in so short a time as that of fifth- and fourth-century Athens. The city of Athens, alone, did not constitute a complete memory place for the individual's experience within a community—that is, it could not unaided embrace the memory of a just leadership as opposed

16. The poignant idea of a "memory place" is sketched throughout Frances Yates' *The Art of Memory*, as the relationship between orderly arrangement in the world and the mind's capacity for memory. See especially pp. 144-145.

to an oppressive one, or the memory of war's romance as opposed to its human cost, or the memory of a court devoted to public discussion of virtue and responsibility as opposed to a court of purely administrative ambitions, or the memory of one man's wisdom and another's reprehensibility. For the transmission of these kinds of judgments, a different sort of memory place had to be revealed —one that would assume the full significance of the city's religious and political heritage without succumbing to its immediate pressures of blind interest and ritual. That new place would reconstitute the city as audience to its own reenacted memory, and would provide the unique opportunity that no other political or cultural form seemed capable of providing: that of acquiring through recollection a human act, by witnessing in drama what one had never lived as one's own. The theatre for the first time would permit past action to be recovered in dramatic performance, and the wisdom or folly of an individual's judgment to belong to the audience's memory, as fastened images of Daedalus, while spectators sat transfixed on seats of stone. And when the performance was finished, all that the city had set out to accomplish might not be lost through time, forgetfulness, and inattention, as the theatre audience emptied onto its city streets.

The first theatre, thus, touched a disquieting nerve in its audiences: mortal existence, entailing successive preparations for certain death, and whose sense of measure was transcendent to itself, had something to teach us in its passing, if we could but remember in time. Consistent with those cultures in Eliade's discussion, Greek culture, too, embraced the normality of suffering. But, in a Heraclitean passion for the structure of opposites in all reality, Aeschylus was sensitive to the positive quality of this suffering. Time, though it be recurrence, does not recur with any exactness. A tragic event might return as farce but never as a specified ancient pattern. The human mind and even time itself begin to acquire a sort of "ontological independence" in Aeschylean theatre.[17] His tragedies emphasize in suffering not its familiarity but its potential lesson. "Pathei mathos," wrote Aeschylus, "one learns through suffering." In J. de Romilly's excellent paraphrase of the *Agamemnon* (180), Aeschylus insisted that "one remembers some cruel experience and the pain feeds on memory; . . . it is remembered in pain . . . [and] even the unwilling then become wise."[18] In time, and for Aeschylus this often bypassed a lifetime, men could derive from the key recollections of terror, defeat, and regret wisdom enough to avert a repetition of their worse catastrophes. This was the slim faith of the new art form, a faith which the peoples of whom Eliade speaks could not have shared.

Having introduced the idea of theatre as recollection, we are left to wonder, then, what was it that these fifth-century Athenians convened to recollect in an excavated hillside? What sorts of urgent questions had newly arisen to be treated in this most public of all arts? In response, we might imagine one of the Dramatic Festival days in the Greek theatre, on which thoughtful spectators filed in to the rhythms of threnody, through the two Parados on either side of the center ground-level stage. Assembled and attending then in silence, they become witnesses to perturbed remembrance. Seated in a half-moon, descending into the hill like a partially exposed tomb, the entire city's population appears collectively to embody its own history, its unconscious, its total inheritance in one earthly, living symbol. With the other half-circle completed by the heavens alone, the theatre itself is the drama, before the performance ever begins. In its very form and silence, it reveals clandestine relations between what is buried and

17. J. de Romilly, *Time in Greek Tragedy*, p. 47.
18. *Ibid.*, pp. 67-68.

must yet be born, from which the words will only struggle outward to consciousness.

The ensuing performance of tragedy at the center of the theatre constitutes, in effect, a mediation between competing claims for human action and their competing audiences: the sacred and the profane.[19] Spheres that had always been discretely mute, one transcendent and the other mundane, were for the first time to be staged in mysterious contact and voice. Those qualities within the provinces of the gods, wisdom and justice, were now to be fruits also of human endeavor, not only in tragic theatre but in the city of its dramatizations. Those urgent questions that Aeschylean theatre would make conscious in the collective memory reflected the most deeply felt needs of collective life, the life of the polis, and were in this sense fundamentally political. Jaeger puts it this way:

The audience, sitting on plain wooden benches about the pounded earth of the round dancing-place, was not already blasé with literature; and the poet by his *psychagogia* could capture the souls of an entire nation in a moment, as no rhapsode had ever done with the poems of Homer. Thus the writer of tragedies was an important political figure; and the state took official cognizance of the art of an elder contemporary of Aeschylus, Phrynichus, when by writing a tragedy on a recent disaster for which the Athenians felt themselves partly responsible—the Persian capture of Miletus—he moved the people to tears.[20]

Verging here on what will be the major focus of the next section, the relationship between theatre and city, it would

19. Otto Rank mentions that the Greeks were the first to establish a purely human-soul concept (as distinct from the Egyptian) by "banishing the dead to below the earth, and the gods to above it"; *Art and Artist*, tr. C. F. Atkinson, p. 169. The Greek theatre's architecture, extending from the ground level to the hilltops, symbolized this mediation between animal-man whose burial place would now be his city—his self-made world—but whose soul would still belong to a universe that could never be humanly controlled and in which it would never be quite at home, despite the new powers of the polis.

20. *Paideia: the Ideals of Greek Culture*, tr. G. Highet, Vol. I, p. 248.

be fruitful rather to pursue the inquiry of what the audience actually witnessed, and the theatre accomplished, in another of its directions. This inquiry imposes itself from the very meaning of the word "theatre," which begins in the ancient Greek verb, "θάομαι": to wonder at, or to gaze upon, look at, to see. From this verb, the word "θέα" gives us the thing seen, the sight or spectacle. Still stressing the objective of *seeing*, the word "θεατρον" (theatron), denoting *a place for seeing*, collectively the spectators, the audience, eventually becomes our word "theatre."[21] Therefore, in its ancient beginnings, the theatre was not defined by the design of its stage, by the elegance of its actors, by its chorus, or even by its haunting lyrics. The theatre was, and has always been, an art dependent for its meaning upon the public's perception and its abilities to remember. First applied to the space occupied by the spectators,[22] the word "theatre" is meant to imply a certain kind of audience: its spectators must learn to see and learn to act in terms of what they see. That is the first purpose of theatre, in its Greek origins as tragedy: to structure the vision of an audience.

That the act of seeing had become problematical is implicit in the very creation of theatre—a place for seeing institutionalized in an art that attempts to assist the "naked" eye. Perhaps the most eloquent and anguished moments of Greek and Shakespearian tragedy rest only on this dilemma: from Oedipus to Lear, one sees how the world goes only when the eyes are gone. For the Greeks, the experience of perception was not limited to the perplexities of physical sight and was never passive, as we discussed above in relation to memory. One's perception comprised "the visual field (the actual retinal image) and the visual

21. Margarete Bieber hints at a deemphasis of insight in public spectacle in the Roman usage of "auditorium." *The History of the Greek and Roman Theaters*, p. 57.
22. Roy C. Flickinger, *The Greek Theater and its Drama*, p. 60.

world"[23] in one whole vision in which the visual world clearly dominated one's ability to physically see. The eye falls on what it expects to discover; in a foreign land, for instance, we can easily eliminate from our visual field an object that is simply unfamiliar. The problem of vision is, then, that it is so often culturally determined that one becomes, in Wittgenstein's striking phrase, "aspect-blind" or the equivalent of colorblind in the total act of seeing beyond mere looking. The theatre attempts to enhance our visual field through exposure to other visual worlds that surpass our limited physical experience, transforming the sight of spectacle into insight. Simply, one perceives what one does not always see, and the visual world is from that moment the same, and never the same again.[24]

We recognize, what is in itself remarkable, that dramatic vision attempts to draw some nobility from the ruins of remembrance. Yet, how is it that theatre endows its audience with this sort of redemption? Once we have been recalled to the event by the tragedian, and even stunned by his words, there is something else, an objectivity that theatre forces upon us because "aside from the spectacle itself the truth is not evident."[25] On the brink of the very performance lies a dimension that transcends the given drama to form a symbolic reality all its own, something Artaud sketches in *The Theater and its Double* and which characterizes the Balinese theatre that inspires it. In fact,

23. This useful distinction is found in E. T. Hall, *The Hidden Dimension*, pp. 78-79.

24. To rest the dilemmas of vision on a concept of the visual world is but the beginning of the problem. For the potential ambiguities of this concept, see Hanna Pitkin's discussion in *Wittgenstein and Justice*, pp. 109-115. In one especially fine example, she writes: "For actions and relationships and feelings and practices and institutions do not walk up to us like elephants and stand there, gently flapping their ears, clearly distinct from their surroundings, waiting to be inspected and named" (p. 115).

25. Leonard C. Pronko, *Theater East and West, Perspectives Toward a Total Theatre*, p. 29.

this elusive reality is achieved by all forms of theatre, when the spectators' awareness of their collective observance and the world of the theatre itself pass into a third universe encompassing them both.

We can take a step in articulating the nature of this passage with the assistance of Susanne Langer's discussion of the art symbol and the "livingness" in all art. She writes, "the art symbol, however, reflects the nature of mind as a culmination of life—and what it directly exhibits, first of all, is the mysterious quality of intangible elements which arise from the growth and activity of the organism, yet do not seem entirely of its substance." "The most powerful means to this end," she suggests, "is the creation of secondary illusions . . . such as . . . the sudden impression of color in music, or of eloquence in the lines of a statue."[26] An example of secondary illusion in the theatre is Francis Fergusson's "timeless moment," the single moment in which one can perceive the destiny of an entire people.[27] Present and future are collapsed, in that instant, into an eternal truth, as they are in Aeschylean visions of private uses of political power and the resulting disintegration of cities. There are few other contexts in which such a timeless moment can be experienced on a public level; in Greek culture, they would all be related to one of the four areas of oratory—forensic, political, dramatic, or elegiac.[28] Some unique instances would be those of extraordinary teaching, true prophecy, and charismatic leadership.

Thus, as if it were too simple, the theatre removes us from "real life" to be in touch with a timeless reality that is never otherwise available in the swamp and tedium of our lives. Witnesses, who are permitted the luxury of observing an action to its completion, gain access to this reality through the baffling power of this art that embraces such

26. Suzanne Langer, *Mind: An Essay on Human Feeling,* Vol. I, pp. 229-230.
27. Langer, p. 240; she refers to Fergusson, *The Idea of a Theater,* p. 193.
28. K. J. Dover, *Greek Popular Morality in the Time of Plato and Aristotle,* p. 5.

enormous complexity and tension without wasting everyone in it, as does life itself. Langer describes this power as
"a division between two states, in which some mysterious
passage or transmutation takes place," and recalling the
timeless moment in drama, she adds: "Action, the mode of
drama, gives way to an inward vision, still on the part of the
agent in the play (not the spectator), but apparent to the
audience as a plastic image would be, though it is not a
visible image. It is poetically created, a mental act of the
dramatic personage that presents itself as though it were
transfixed in a sort of mental space."[29]

Taking our cue from Langer's phrase "a division between two states," the quintessence of theatre moves into
sharper relief. For this ability to tolerate hopeless divisions,
this unmarked crossroads, this homing-place for unsus-
pected connections is what so characterizes the theatre. Its
stage cannot keep things apart and cannot fuse them together; exposing them, in their interstices, as they are in
life left unexposed: totally related in their separateness
and totally inseparable. It is not merely that in its Greek
beginnings, theatre brought men, women, children, slaves,
and prisoners into a single forum at the same moment, but
that each aspect of the city's existence—historical, economic, social, political, religious, scientific—was brought to
mind. If E. M. Forster was not thinking of the theatre when
he quoted, in preface to *Howard's End,* the words "only
connect," it was his novel's good fortune to enlist dramatic
art's ancient purpose.

The study of theatre's principal divisions or tensions,
which begins with Hegel's "collision," eventually leads us to
the identification of three that are universal to all theatre,
whether it be African, Asian, or European of origin. These
tensions are treated in differing emphasis and interpretation, but in finding theatre uniquely congenial for their

29. Langer, *Mind,* p. 240.

difficult reenactment, they are preserved as the following: the tension between consciousness and the unconscious, between self and community, and between the political and the religious (the public and the transcendent). All forms of theatre carry these thematic contradictions simultaneously, effecting a bridge between irreconcilable regions within the psyche and within the world, and between both of these and the past. The audiences of theatre are then transported across this bridge, upon an often unwanted inward journey of the soul toward its responsibilities. Unwanted, because as Marx said long after the first appearance of Greek theatre, "the tradition of all the dead generations weighs like a nightmare on the brain of the living."[30]

The first of these tensions, between consciousness and the unconscious, receives some special attention here while the main body of this work centers on dialectics of the other two. Of course, in dramatic performance as in life, there is no facile delineation between them, and my intention here is rather to speak to the larger sensibilities of the art form before plunging into specific instances of it in Aeschylus, Shakespeare, and Brecht. For theatre, in addition to its functions as *memory place* and *a place for seeing*, is bound by its passion for unities in a visual universe that is perpetually fragmented. Thus the current predilection to see the planet's diverse cultures as three different worlds in some sort of hierarchy would not be a vision of theatre, which has always addressed itself to a whole universe in a passion for transmuting divisions. Whether this core of unity can ever be realized in the lives of persons or histories of cities, it lives on in the theatre, whose art translates the fleeting experiences of its different spectators into a single public recollection.

Confirming other applications of universality, one writer

30. Karl Marx, *The 18th Brumaire of Louis Bonaparte* (International Publishers, New York, 1963), p. 15.

establishes a parallel between dreams in the mental experience of an individual and works of art in any society, calling the latter "manifestations of a collective dream."[31] He means by this, in part, what we have been discussing as the problem of vision in all theatre. The collective dream dramatizes the society's concealed states of psychic tension, to enable the perception and evaluation of human action within social contexts that would appear to be discrete. More specifically, he concludes, "organic relations are thus implied between historical circumstances, psychic states, and forms of cultural expression."[32] Theatre's audience confronts the task of rescuing from the rubble of its collective memory implicit ordering principles for the whole of its political and spiritual existence. It is equally obsessed with the possibilities of undiscovered worlds and empires lost. This is why the theatre often thrives as tragedy within a nation confident of its future aspirations. In tragic consciousness, the future is only a haunted backward glance, a place like the theatre itself where one is ensnared in the grip of past truths. One hopes only that action will have acquired a few ordering principles, that it will be confined to some stage of meaning, and that it will tell a story worthy of repetition.

In brief, the theatre sets out to thwart our most common expectations, summoning us from their crude engineering of memory into the abyss of mistaken assumptions that precedes a genuine insight. It is an art form devoted to a vision of inward order, which its first audiences not only witnessed but attempted to comprehend within their own political foundations. As we shall see, the concept of political form is paramount and problematic in all tragedy; political form reflects a changing universe which, in the absence of theatre, is difficult to grasp in its entirety, as it must be grasped in order to endow human acts with

31. Walter Abell, *The Collective Dream in Art*, p. 5.
32. *Ibid.*, p. 54.

understandable purpose. The unusual polity that submits to the scrutinies of theatre is cognizant of the intimate bonds between dramatic and political action and of the need for art's presentations to sustain ideals of human liberation that are the source of all human creativity and the very desire for life itself. In this vein, Victor Ehrenberg has written, "the theatre *was* the Polis."[33] What he meant by this, and what we must draw from it, are the concerns of the following discussion on the origins of Greek tragedy.

33. *Sophocles and Pericles,* p. 6.

2. Theatron, Polis, and Thanatos

From about the year 535 B.C., when Peisistratus founded theatre as an institution in Athens, until 404 B.C., the date recorded by Thucydides as the end of the Peloponnesian War, there flourished the ancient city of Athens and within it the first theatre for tragedy.[1] Much has been written on the origins of Greek tragedy, but a tendency to neglect the political nature of both city and theatre has frozen the harvest of much of this writing.[2] Apparently little curiosity has been drawn from one simple and obvious fact: the theatre and the city came into being together for the first time in history and suffered simultaneous disintegration. Any discussion of the origins of tragedy has at least to deal with this conjunction of circumstances. Severed from the city, the theatre would seem to be disembodied.

The most conventional interpretation of the origins of Greek tragedy, from Nietzsche to Gilbert Murray, has emphasized an alleged antagonism between tragic drama and political order itself. Where the city is structure, order, and reason, we are told, the theatre is its antithesis. This romantic view of the theatre, as opposed in essence to all that is political, might be stirring but is without substance, and the objective of what follows here will be to supplant it with a

1. See the discussion of Peisistratus in Gerald F. Else, *The Origin and Early Form of Greek Tragedy,* p. 49; and in J. T. Sheppard, *Aeschylus, the Prophet of Greek Freedom,* p. 5.

2. There are significant exceptions to this, and I am especially indebted to the insightful research in anthropology and archeology in relation to Greek tragedy done at the turn of the century by William Ridgeway and later Jane Ellen Harrison. Essentially, I am not offering a new theory of the origins, but rather combining some findings of anthropology with a political reevaluation of the art form's meaning.

different vision of the theatre, as suggested by the society
and culture of its origins and by the first great tragedian
himself, Aeschylus. First, a look at the troubled legacy from
Nietzsche.

It is important at the outset to make two serious qualifications of what will be said in criticism of Nietzsche's *Birth of
Tragedy*: no sweeping censure of Nietzsche's thought as a
whole is intended; and Nietzsche's interpretation was not
so much wrong as it was partial.[3] As with soil unevenly
tilled, seeds bear fruit here and there. It is for us to sift
through what remains to see where Nietzsche might have
led us astray. There are three specific formulations in *The
Birth of Tragedy* that do not fit the evidence, such as it now
stands. These are: (a) that tragedy in its origins excludes
any kind of social or political context; (b) that Aeschylean
use of the chorus was strictly Dionysian; and (c) that the
essence of *Prometheus Bound* and Aeschylus' plays in general was Dionysian wisdom, meaning "the end of individu-
ation."[4] Objections to these three statements are not mutually exclusive. In one sense, this entire discussion is addressed to the first of them. However, the key element in all
Nietzsche has to say about the birth of tragedy is its alleged
"Dionysian" foundations, so it is best to begin with the
problem of Dionysos and its relationship to the origins of
theatre, if this relationship ever existed.

There is a study sufficiently complete in its treatment of
Nietzsche and Dionysos in terms of the specific points
raised here that I will only try to reinforce some of its major
conclusions. Gerald F. Else in his *The Origin and Early Form
of Greek Tragedy*[5] reminds us that the entire testimony of
Dionysiac ritual is quite thin, even in terms of ritual performance, but its link with the origin of drama is nonexis-

3. Francis Fergusson claims Nietzsche's views have been superseded and "in the
light of subsequent investigations, look nightmarishly partial and distorted." *Idea
of a Theater*, pp. 100-101.

4. Nietzsche, *The Birth of Tragedy*, tr. F. Golffing, pp. 47-67.

5. Else, p. 5.

tent, except for Aristotle's *Poetics*,[6] which gives us the version of tragedy as derived from "the dithyramb: that is, the cult of Dionysos," often with accompanying goat-like satyrs.[7] Nietzsche's *Birth of Tragedy*, according to Else, "does not present any new theory of the origin; it simply visualizes, visionalizes, an outline of events suggested in Aristotle's *Poetics*."[8] Nietzsche retains Aristotle's rendering of the origins, but he imposes upon Aristotle's sense of dithyramb—which was "a lyric presentation of heroic subjects, not a specifically Dionysiac performance"—the consuming distraction of Dionysian trance.[9] Whatever Nietzsche's philosophical intentions and purposes were, we must reconstruct the pale history of Dionysos with respect to tragedy by tracing the history of Dionysos in relation to the dithyramb itself.

Most available scholarly research has determined that Dionysos is not related to the dithyramb, let alone to theatre, until quite late in Attic history, around the end of the sixth century B.C. Pickard-Cambridge, reviewing this question of the dithyramb in the 1930s, saw that the problem of linking Dionysos with the dithyramb begins with the first mention of dithyramb, from Archilochus of Paros during the first half of the seventh century B.C. "There is no assurance that the dithyramb in later sixth-century Dionysiac festivals at Athens . . . was really an alien accretion." His concluding discussion of the dithyramb reveals that "no complete dithyramb, except those of Bacchylides (if they are dithyrambs) survives."[10] And he concludes: "Our evidence for the early history of tragedy is so slight that any account is unsatisfactory. . . . The *Persae* already has all the solemnity and grandeur of Aeschylean tragedy. It is difficult to see a thread leading back from

---

6. See Else's major work, *Aristotle's Poetics,* for a complete analysis.
7. Else, *The Origin and Early Form of Greek Tragedy,* p. 12.
8. *Ibid.,* p. 10.
9. *Ibid.,* pp. 13-14.
10. Pickard-Cambridge, *Dithyramb, Tragedy and Comedy,* pp. 1, 58.

here to a performance of fat men and satyrs."[11] From Pickard-Cambridge's analysis, it has been highly doubtful for some time that any association of the dithyramb and Dionysos can be supported by Attic history. This, of course, flatly undermines the influence Dionysos could conceivably have had upon the origins of tragedy, even if Dionysian ritual was later imported into Athenian culture.

In retrospect, it is odd that Aristotle introduced these troublesome satyrs and goat-men into the discussion of the dithyramb if, indeed, he meant that term to refer to a more sober learning experience. Returning to Else's analysis, we are warned that the appearance of the satyr in Aristotle's version is part of the muddle created by certain writers attempting to "superimpose a pre-history of tragedy in the Peloponnese upon a history in Attica which is complete and coherent in itself. . . . It stems from an attempt by certain 'Dorians' in the later fourth century B.C. to annex the origins of both tragedy and comedy."[12] Thus, we find Aristotle asserting on etymological grounds that the Dorians invented tragic theatre because choral odes in Attic tragedy were all in the Doric dialect. William Ridgeway has shown, however, that these were not Doric forms but old Attic, and points out that Aristotle studied tragedy with slight interest in its beginnings, focusing rather upon its fully developed form. Devoting, then, little careful analysis to tragedy's origins, Aristotle's account is often ambiguous. In one place, he claims that tragedy arose out of Doric satyric drama, while in another place (*Poetics*, IV), he writes: "When Tragedy and Comedy came to light, the two classes of poets still followed their natural bent; the lampooners became writers of Comedy, and the Epic poets were succeeded by Tragedians, since the drama was a larger and higher form of art."[13]

11. *Ibid.*, pp. 130-131.
12. Else, *The Origin*, p. 21.
13. Quoted in Ridgeway, *The Origin of Tragedy*, p. 57.

Ridgeway's own excellent discussion of the origins of tragedy discloses other fundamental aspects of the Dionysos-dithyramb question which relate those origins to the meaning of death in Greek religion. Several of his conclusions are compelling and warrant our particular attention. First, long before the appearance of the Thracian cult god Dionysos, initiatory rites and mimetic dancing existed in the Peloponnese. The Athenians regarded Dionysos as exogenous to their own culture, and in coming to adopt him they created what Ridgeway calls a "double cult." That is, at least since Homeric times, they had worshipped dead heroes in athletic feats, contests of horsemanship, and tragic dances in order to appease or honor the dead. This worship of the dead is evident in the *Iliad,* from Achilles' lamentation for Patrocles, for example, and is evident in the Peloponnese area in celebrations honoring Adrastus at Sicyon and Iolaus at Thebes before the Dorian invasions of 1104 B.C.[14] Other cultures have shared, and continue to exemplify, this particular ritual worship with respect to the dead. Attila, for instance, was attended in death by the following Hunnish spectacle and rites:

The body was placed in a silken pavilion. . . . Horsemen, the flower of the Huns, riding around the spot where the king lay, uttering funeral laments, and recalling his exploits; how Attila, foremost of the Huns, son of Mundzuccus, was the lord of most valiant nations; how with power unheard of before his day he became sole master of the kingdoms of Scythia and Germany; how by capturing cities he had struck terror into the Eastern and Western empires . . . how after he had accomplished all this with unchequered good fortune, he had fallen not by the enemy's sword, nor by the treachery of his followers, but when his people were in full enjoyment of peace and prosperity. . . . Who would call this death! When they had thus bewailed and lamented him to the full, they held over his grave-mound a funeral feast . . . in which pleasure and grief were strangely commingled.[15]

14. *Ibid.,* p. 67.
15. *Ibid.,* pp. 34-35.

This spectacle reflected a long-standing belief that the dead would enjoy the same activities as in life, and that their spirits could be recalled by the reenactment of their past deeds. One can imagine how formidable such a hero would be in the recollections of choral lament. Indeed, it was as if he still lived, still ruled, and was impervious to time and change in the world.

In addition to commemorating a great personage, festivals were created to avenge a wrong-doing (the theme of Orestes in Aeschylus' *Libation Bearers*, and that of *Hamlet*), or out of guilt for a transgression. In time, every local town and village in Greece had its own hero and festival held at the burial site. Traditional offerings of cakes were laid at the tomb, and rites were organized in such a way as to propitiate the dead person whose spirit, it was believed, dwelled near the grave.[16] Communication between living and dead was believed essential to the future well-being of the land, for to abandon the dead was far worse than death itself, which was but a state of dumbness or sleep. Only forgetfulness, and not death, could deprive a people of its own distinctive identity. If not held in memory, the departed ancestor was not merely dead; it was as if he or she had never existed. No culture can bear the thought that it will leave no trace on the earth, that nothing of one's life will last among the living beyond the final breath, whether or not there is a conception of the afterlife.[17]

Then, Greek towns begin to adopt a double cult, Ridgeway explains, when the local hero's festival acquires a well-known deity as well, like Zeus, Apollo, Poseidon, Hermes,

16. Ridgeway, *The Early Age of Greece*, Vol. I, p. 512.
17. Philippe Aries has shown, with respect to this, that monuments to the dead have traditionally been a visible sign of the city's permanence. *Western Attitudes Toward Death: From the Middle Ages to the Present*, tr. P. Ranum, p. 74. If the theatre has developed, as we are suggesting, from epic and ritual honoring the dead at the tomb, the theatre's meaning as a memory place in which to contemplate past heroes would have an intimate relationship to the city's own well-being and perpetuation. There is a lasting connection between the city's endurance as a political entity and its being perpetuated in memory through dramatic art.

Athena, or Dionysos. The former tomb, in these instances, becomes also a fire-altar—fire, because the fumes would be carried up to the gods, whereas libations for heroes were placed upon or poured directly into the grave. The *thymele* (combination tomb and fire-altar) appeared together with the first Greek tragic chorus, on the stage and in the orchestra of the theatre.[18] The question here that pertains to the origins of tragedy, is which cult came first in Attica: the worship of the dead, or the worship of Dionysos? Ridgeway shows that for generations, there had been festivals honoring the dead or related to the harvest each month of the year, and that the months were, in fact, named for these festivals. Two festivals were named for Dionysos—the Country Dionysia in December, and the Great or City Dionysia in April—but no month bears the name of Dionysos. Therefore, he concludes that these festivals precede Dionysos and were later named for the newly acquired Dionysian cult from Thrace. One interesting hypothesis as to the Athenian adoption of Dionysos is that Cleisthenes (grandfather of the Athenian ruler) first brought the cult into Sicyon in order to overshadow the great dead hero, Adrastus, thereby reinforcing his own power over the local populace—in other words, for political reasons.[19] The year of Dionysos' introduction into Sicyon cannot have been earlier than 600 B.C., and Thespis had most likely been composing and presenting tragic choruses since 570 B.C. From Suidas, we learn that at least fifteen composers of tragedy even precede Thespis' creative period (570-535), one of whom was Epigenes of Sicyon, who was engrossed in his artistic labors at a time when the cult of Dionysos was not even known to his city. Thespis himself did not leave traces of Dionysian themes in his own tragedies.[20]

---

18. Ridgeway, *Origin of Tragedy*, pp. 39-47.
19. *Ibid.*, pp. 67-68.
20. *Ibid.*, pp. 68-69.

This leads to Ridgeway's second conclusion: the Dionysos that the Athenians ultimately preserved had undergone their own idiosyncratic interpretation. The only "pure" Dionysian element in Athenian theatre would have been the satyr drama, but this was introduced by Pratinus in the early fifth century after the first presentations of tragic choruses and was drawn largely from their materials. Even the Dionysos in Euripides is not at all the original "rude and coarse" Thracian god. In this respect, Ridgeway concludes: "Thus even that which had once been the true Dionysiac element faded before the national instincts of the Athenians, and with the invention of melodrama by Euripides and the rise of true comedy it finally disappeared altogether."[21]

Third and finally, Ridgeway argues that the dithyramb hymns from which tragedy did emerge were hymns to celebrate the dead hero and were primarily solemn accompaniments to the ritual held at his tomb; they were not in any remote sense "licentious vintage songs."[22] Moreover, hymns honoring the dead, out of which tragedy eventually was created, are to be found in scattered areas all over the world. Ritual presentations still bearing a resemblance to early Greek mimetic rituals may be found in the ancient Hindu drama (the Ramayana), the sacred plays of Tibet and Mongolia, the Malay drama, and the drama of the Veddas of Ceylon. Ridgeway concludes, in view of these similarities, "it would appear that the principle from which Tragedy sprang was not confined to Greece or to Mediterranean lands, but is world-wide and one of the many touches that make the whole world kin."[23]

With this, he sustains one of the main themes of this study: that whatever the peculiar political and social environments within which theatre has developed, and whatever the subtle poetic inspirations that go into the creation

21. *Ibid.*, pp. 53-55.
22. *Ibid.*, p. 38.
23. *Ibid.*, p. 108.

of this rare art form, the urge to create it persists and will become manifest in many places on the earth where the dilemmas of political order and the acceptance of organic cycles and death are still public preoccupations. The significant connection that must be inferred from Ridgeway's analysis is that the epic narratives, festivals, and choral chants that ultimately became the first drama are rooted in the *transformation of death into a public ceremony*.[24] Not Dionysos but *Thanatos* haunts the collective memory that gives birth to theatre.

In light of the foregoing, one would have to reject Dionysian ritual as the origin of the dithyramb that ultimately passed from the early efforts of Thespis into the mature tragedies of Aeschylus. Given Pickard-Cambridge's admission that the evidence is incomplete at best, heroic epic myths and their rituals *are* the most convincing sources for tragic drama. Yet if the conventional theory from Aristotle to Nietzsche is discounted as unsatisfactory, still the question remains, how did theatre emerge from the public ceremonies of death surrounding the tomb? What was the impetus for the creation of drama, and how is it related to the city? Two scholars following Ridgeway have offered fresh and imaginative answers in the first quarter of this century: Jane Ellen Harrison and F. M. Cornford. Harrison, in her study of the dithyramb and early drama, begins by asking *why* a group of people should try to represent itself through collective or individual action or acting. She discovers at first a psychological impetus to amend the memory of fruitless past action by making sense of it in the structure of a plot or story; and soon this is translated into the need for a new birth or new beginning on the level of the whole group or society in the reenacting of past action.

24. Philippe Aries speaks of death as a public ceremony until the time of our own century, in which it becomes a forbidden event, in *Western Attitudes Toward Death*, pp. 12, 104-107: "Death was the awareness by each person of a *Destiny* in which his own personality was not annihilated but put to sleep—*requies, dormitio*. This *requies* presupposed a survival. . . . On both sides of death, one is still very near the deep wellsprings of sentiment" (p. 104).

As Hannah Arendt has noted, the Greeks believed that "men, though they must die, are not born in order to die but in order to begin."[25] This reenactment or "representation," as it was first understood, was intended to prove that "such and such *really did happen*."[26] The group could believe in itself—that it *had acted*—and take responsibility for its identity and meaning *as a whole*, and in this way could begin a new life.

From this thoroughly unique conception of ritual representation, the group makes a simple leap from the particular to the universal. "What happened" becomes "what happens." The representative action which began as commemorative develops into an ideal or lesson for future action. Cornford brings this line of thought to a poignant conclusion: "The first religious representation is a representation of the collective consciousness itself—the only moral power which can come to be felt as imposed from without, and therefore need to be represented. . . . From its positive content come . . . strange as it may seem, that idea of 'nature' which lies at the root of philosophy."[27] So primary is the idea of collective and political form in early representation in Greek art that even the concept of nature, and eventually of the Divine, which the fertility ritual so passionately celebrates, owes its meaning first to it. Cornford remarks ironically, "The eternal laws, of which Antigone said that no one knew from whence they were proclaimed, can now be seen to have been projected, as a sort of Brocken spectre, from those very laws of the state with which she contrasts them."[28]

From this discussion of political order and the concept of nature, one can discern a cardinal element in the creation of tragedy. Cornford adds that Plato's entire quarrel with the doctrine of atomism was based upon his conviction that

25. *The Human Condition,* p. 222.
26. J. E. Harrison, *Themis,* p. 44 (emphasis mine).
27. *From Religion to Philosophy,* p. 82.
28. *Ibid.,* p. 54.

"the State is natural and, if reconstructed on ideal lines, might embody the same principles of justice that rule through every part of the cosmos."[29] This radically new conviction that political order in the world is *natural* to men—that is, appropriate to the needs of the human soul—constitutes the preface to tragic theatre. Of itself, it cannot account for the birth of tragedy, and yet it cannot be sufficiently emphasized.[30] It denotes the relationship between a bountiful faith in the constructive powers of attachment, memory, and identity on the one hand and the idea of political order on the other, as well as the need to project the problematical contradictions and limitations of political life through dramatic art. Tragedy has, for this reason, been best captured in the phrase, a "polity play."[31]

The Athenian who, before Aeschylus, underscores this idea of the polity as a natural home for man is Solon.[32] It was he who first urged the acceptance of the collective responsibility for the acts of the city.[33] There would be no blame cast upon the gods for what was the rightful jurisdiction of human law and reason. Solon even denied Athenians a Spartan dependence upon the military in political matters. Only the people in collective contemplation and judgment could arrive at social justice. Solon's most significant single innovation for tragic theatre seems to have been a public reading of his "Salamis" poem, which marked the first occasion poetry was used in a dialogue between poet and citizens, during a situation of political crisis to,

29. *Ibid.*, p. 183.

30. By the time we are confronted in Europe and America with the age of Lockean liberalism, for which political order is deemed not merely unnatural to man but an obliged minimal constraint for the sake of individual privacy, the whole project of tragedy is nearly inconceivable. That a man is an autonomous individual prevents him from ever encountering the torment of Hegel's "tragic collision."

31. Richard Kuhns, *The House, the City, and the Judge,* p. 139.

32. See Else's chapter entitled "Solon and Peisistratus," in *The Origin,* and M. H. Scharlemann, "The Influences of the Social Changes in Athens on the Development of Greek Tragedy."

33. See Ivan M. Linforth, *Solon the Athenian.*

influence the immediate action of those citizens.[34] With
the innovations of Solon in the sixth century, and as the
community and political order are recognized as primary
and natural, order becomes simultaneously problematic.
Thoughtful citizens begin to accuse their own political
arrangements of injustice. They grow all at once impatient
with social and economic inequities they had endured for
centuries. The awareness that some men will value life
because of their social conditions while others will long for
death to end the miseries of their existence produced, in
Greek tragedy, a sorrow that was as much political as exis-
tential: a sorrow that an environment humanly conceived
can narrow and foreclose human chances for purpose and
meaning in life as much, or more, than the arbitrary gods
or the devastations of earthquakes. A theme is launched in
this century that will receive the most compassionate poetic
statement in *Prometheus Bound* and will find its way to the
pen of Karl Marx some twenty-three centuries later.[35] It
was apparent to Solon and to Thespis that if we are responsible for our political arrangements and institutions, we can
make them either better or worse for those who are subject
to them. And so the question which has become a common-
place of political theory arose in the twilight hours of
theatre's commencement: what is the best political arrangement or form within which all people might live?

Similarly, the pre-Socratics, notably Heraclitus, become
preoccupied with rational systems to aid their comprehension of an uncertain universe. There is a strange self-
confidence born of the need for a rational but paradoxical
approach: both the uncertainty of a reasonable universe
and the certainty of having to use reason. André Malraux

34. Else, *The Origin*, p. 41.
35. Marx wrote in his 1844 manuscripts: "The dwelling full of light which
Aeschylus' Prometheus indicates as one of the great gifts by which he has changed
savages into men, ceases to exist for the worker. . . . None of his senses exist any
longer, either in a human form, or even in a non-human, animal form." *Karl Marx,
Early Writings,* tr. & ed. T. B. Bottomore (McGraw-Hill Paperbacks, N.Y., 1963),
pp. 169-170.

beautifully illustrates the effect this paradox had upon Greek art in his *La Musée Imaginaire*, and shows how it distinguished the Greek from other art. There persisted the haunting presence of a human world in which no just order seemed possible, but in which the vision of order (the polis) was as real as the chaos (the Erinyes of Aeschylean drama) that overtakes it. Tragedy draws its vision from the possibilities of order that do not materialize. All that remained for the first appearance of tragic theatre in the mid-sixth century was for Thespis to introduce this element into actual dramatic performance by combining the heroic myths of Homer and others with the teachings of Solon.

The pain and displacement of the "common man" were uniquely dramatized by Thespis in the form of a chorus composed of citizens. The chorus and a single actor were made to represent the people confronting their leader or hero. As Ridgeway suggests, this must have been received with amazement by the sixth-century Athenians, for it was Thespis who first dramatized the myths of dead heroes no longer near their own tombs or shrines, as had been the custom for generations, but far away from their own graves.[36] To Thespis, the examples conveyed by these heroes greatly surpassed the comforts of local saints, and encompassed all men's responsibilities in political life. This seemingly small step was another essential moment in the creation of theatre. With this new confrontation, tragedy represented, in effect, "the beginning of a new spiritual unification of Attica."[37] The new Greek theatre, in architecture and in meaning, thus symbolized the city's graveyard—in the sense that it was a place where the spirit of the past could be recalled, action in the present informed, and the city's identity perpetuated. (See accompanying figure.)

36. Ridgeway, *Origin of Tragedy*, p. 62. Philippe Aries helps us understand this key link in the development of drama from the public worship of the dead: "The important element was the calling to mind of the deceased's identity, and not the remembrance of the exact place where the body had been placed," in *Western Attitudes Toward Death*, p. 50.

37. Else, *The Origin*, p. 76.

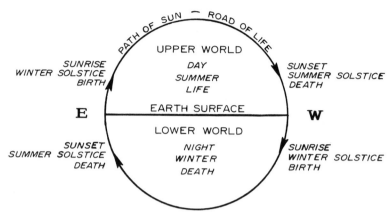

The Hopi conception of life and death is sketched above. If one imagines it to be a drawing of the Greek theatre instead, the audience would be seated in the lower half-circle, symbolically occupying the city's tomb or burial site. From this lower world, the historical past, ancestors, and collective memory would be recollected in the dramatic performance that would bring the dead to life, memories to consciousness, once again on the earthen stage. Between the upper world of the present actors and the lower world of the symbolic past, would stand the chorus, whose function is to give collective voice to the memories stirred in the audience, in a way that contributes to the new tragic vision being constructed before them. Theatre, then, does become the city—the city of its past, a city of the dead—to evoke in memory an awareness of self and community that only the moment of death itself seems capable of eliciting from us. (Hopi Figure, "The Road of Life," from Frank Waters, *Book of the Hopi*, Ballantine Books, Inc., New York, 1963, p. 231, drawing by Oswald White Bear Fredericks.)

Karl Jaspers, in composing his thoughts on tragedy after the Second World War, wrote, "Tragedy occurs whenever awareness exceeds power; and particularly where awareness of a major need exceeds the power to satisfy it."[38] Likewise, we find the Athenians entering upon their fifth century with the awareness of collective memory, of political and social injustices, and of the problematical aspects of the city's form with its powers to shape the destinies of men,

38. *Tragedy Is Not Enough*, p. 17.

and with no answer except that of the sober, tense, and tragic dramas of Aeschylus. Indeed, the word for "actor" was at first the word "answerer."

The more one seeks to clarify the initial steps in the creation of tragic theatre, the more one becomes immersed in the foundations of the city itself, the center of collective life, and its search for justice. We have seen both that a vast heritage of heroic epic myths and ritual celebrations precede the emergence of tragic theatre; and that the city, which itself is being oriented and developed simultaneously, takes on the tragic objective of constituting man's most natural setting. This was what Aristotle meant, of course, when he said that man was by nature a political animal (a citizen of the polis); not because he acquired this nature simply by being born within the city's walls, but because he aspired to a human nature that only life within the polis could eventually grant him. This is our prelude to the theatre, a public institution that first attempted to portray the tragic proportions of its city's aspirations.

In the course of the centuries in which the classical city of Athens and its theatre for tragedy ran their life-lines, there were no major political events that did not find their way to some corner of the earthen stage for tragedy. The tragedian was the acknowledged teacher of the polis, and his vocation was so grounded in the city's existence that his very name confirmed it; he was called τραγωδο-πολος, the city's playwright. It was essential to the first tragedians, and equally important for us, to understand that the theatre was a constant though sometimes harsh companion to its new city—a city eager for economic prosperity through expansion, a city anxious at first to see itself as a whole and later intent upon being the unseen actor in its own self-destructive policies.[39] Through it all, the first

39. A. W. H. Adkins remarks that it was only after the Persian wars that many Greek cities began to consider the freedom of Greece as a whole. Aeschylus' *The Persians* would have had an obvious impact upon this new political perception in Athens. *Moral Values and Political Behavior in Ancient Greece*, p. 58.

theatre for tragedy endured to record, to warn, to criticize, to remind, and to envision. Before moving on to explore the Aeschylean mastery of these dramatic capacities, a brief examination follows of the political and social contexts of the theatre and its relationship to the city of Athens around the first years of the fifth century.

The early history of Attica would indicate that the theatre is not an accident in a society's development. Environmental conditions seemed to favor the outcome; for example, Attica developed much more slowly than Asia Minor, Corinth, or the surrounding areas, benefiting from its neighbors' errors.[40] From Miletus, in particular, it was able to extract three major concepts—the polis, the kosmos, and the individual—and to combine them patiently in an aging process for enhanced quality. More immediately, the social composition of Attica and the Athenian Council (the Boule) were significantly reshaped during the rule of Cleisthenes, around 508 B.C. According to Plutarch, Solon founded the first Boule of 400 members representing the four major tribes of the area. Because this arrangement permitted conservative landowners too much political influence, Cleisthenes devoted his skills of maneuver to dividing the old clan alliances and effecting a new supremacy of urban interests in Athens over those of rural Attica. He accomplished this by establishing ten new tribes, and expanding the Boule's membership to 500, consisting of fifty members from each of the newly established tribes.[41]

The broader distribution of social classes within each tribe expanded its former local peripheries and encouraged a sense of city-wide loyalty which for the first time exceeded that of the more parochial tribal loyalty. Cleisthenes' Boule represented every part of Attica and undertook the responsibility of presenting all major business to the Assembly, which included every male citizen.[42] This

40. Scharlemann, "Influences of Social Changes," p. 40.
41. P. J. Rhodes, *The Athenian Boule*, pp. 1-13.
42. C. M. Bowra, *Periclean Athens*, pp. 13-14.

welding together of the city's interests altered the complexion of the Athenian theatre's audiences, which were now predominantly urban and involved directly in the political life of Athens. It has been estimated that during Cleisthenes' rule, one-third of the citizens served on the Boule at some period during their lives.[43] Most Athenian citizens attended approximately forty ordinary meetings of the Assembly in a single year. This provided obvious groundwork for Aeschylus' view of political responsibility as a thing shared, and that the final tragic actor is always the city itself (as in the *Suppliants* and the *Eumenides*).

Preceding Cleisthenes' reforms, Peisistratus and Thespis initiated the Dramatic Festivals at Athens around 535 B.C., in the spring festival of the Great or City Dionysia. The first performances were probably in the marketplace, the Agora, but after the wooden benches that had been erected for spectators apparently collapsed in the 70th Olympiad (498 B.C.), the hillside theatre of stone was gradually constructed between the Acropolis and the Odeum of Agrippa.[44] In the two annual religious festivals at Athens, drama was performed for six hours or so a day for several days consecutively.[45] One must try to imagine the kind of commitment that would sustain an audience composed of most of the city's population for that duration. Both the selection of judges for the tragedies and the financing of the theatre confirm, as well, the centrality of the Dramatic Festival in the Athenian polis. The judges, who would determine the merits of the competing dramas, had to represent the entire citizenry and were chosen for their reputed incorruptibility in public life. The city's way of insuring this was to accept a list of names from each of the ten tribes in the Boule; each list was subsequently sealed in an urn. Anyone who broke the seals before the contests began was charged with a capital offense. On the first day of the performances,

43. Aristotle, *Constitution of Athens*, tr. von Fritz and Kapp, XX–XXII.
44. Bieber, *The History of the Greek and Roman Theaters*, p. 54.
45. D. W. Lucas, *The Greek Tragic Poets*, p. 1.

the ten urns were brought to the theatre and opened. The "Archon drew one name from each, and the ten thus chosen swore to give an impartial verdict."[46]

The minimum estimate of an Athenian audience, including perhaps thousands of foreign visitors, is about 17,000 persons. Admission to the theatre was a third of a drachma per day for guests; during Pericles' rule, Athenian citizens were admitted without fee. The rich were honored to sponsor the best tragedians as their choregos, but the essential burden was carried by the state, "the assumption [being] that drama is the community's concern, as we think education is today."[47] Thus, the relationship between the polis and its theatron is an accepted and fundamental fact of its entire existence as a polity. The theatre was directly administered by the city from the time of Peisistratus and even fully funded by it under Pericles.

Now perhaps, Victor Ehrenberg's allusion to the identity of theatre and polis begins to push through the fine metaphor to the heart of the matter. For, upon its mortal landscape, the city of Athens was to wage its campaigns of power extraction and imposition in the "real world," while the city that was the theatre would bear the weight of spiritual restraint, precautions of foresight, and the despair of a disjunction between the city that acts and the city that would see. To sum up in a single vision, the theatre was to the city "a kingdom of the dead corresponding to that of the living."[48] Thus the difference between action as art in the theatre, and action as politics in the city, was the difference between action that had been created from the dead and action that could still lead to death in the future.

46. H. C. Baldry, *The Greek Tragic Theatre*, pp. 25-27.
47. *Ibid.*, p. 31.
48. Otto Rank, *Art and Artist*, p. 293.

3. Political Education Through Tragedy

In the absence of reliable records, many biographical portraits of famous figures in the classical age have all the lethal charm of gossip. This, in any event, is often the case with Aeschylus. What we know of him, we know from his extant works and the anonymous *Life*, composed in the fourth and third centuries B.C., edited at the Alexandrian Library, and containing essentially "the written reminiscences of contemporaries, accounts of his dramatic technique and the personalia of his life . . . passing references in later authors, and the oral tradition."[1] The dating is always haphazard; a man's birthdate is presumed to be from forty to fifty years before his first public recognition. The Parian Marble makes Aeschylus 35 at the battle of Marathon, in 490, and 69 at the time of his death in 456 or 455. His birth is assumed to be 525, at Eleusis, "of the nobility."[2] He fought also at Salamis and possibly at Plataea, and at least one of his brothers was slain by the Persians at Marathon.

We do not know when Aeschylus began writing tragedy, perhaps around 500, but he was his own choreographer and actor as well as dramatist. According to the Parian Marble, he did not win his first victory until the spring of 484.[3] He composed at least seventy dramas and five satyr plays and received at least thirteen victories, of which only five have survived to the twentieth century: *The Persians,*

---

1. Anthony J. Podlecki, *The Political Background of Aeschylean Tragedy*, p. 3.
2. *Ibid.*, p. 3; note, pp. 153-154.
3. *Ibid.*, p. 5.

Seven Against Thebes, The Suppliants, Oresteia, and *Prometheus Bound.*[4] He died in Gela, Sicily; a bizarre story attached to his death has it that he was killed by an eagle who, mistaking the poet's bald head for a rock, dropped a tortoise on it to break the shell.[5] Whether this folktale is meant to convey that he suffered an accident, or whether it is an Athenian form of "cover-up," is part of the arcanum surrounding his departure from Athens and his subsequent death.

For the man's character, beliefs, and moods, we have his own incomparable work. A careful appreciation of his plays affirms their author's philosophical seriousness, devotion to the critical perception of his audience, faith in the high quality of human potential, an awe of political power, and an obsession with extraordinary political leadership. Unlike Sophocles, his face was wide and stern, sparing him the refined, softer lines; there was in his countenance something foreboding. Ironically, the Athenian who bears the most striking resemblance to him, in both mood and theoretical conceptions, is the philosopher often thought to have advocated the elimination of tragedy, Plato.[6] We will return to this comparison during discussions of the *Eumenides* and *Prometheus Bound.*

One of the more revealing stories that comes down to us about Aeschylus is from Plutarch and attributed to Ion of Chios: "When Aeschylus was a spectator at the Isthmian

4. *Ibid.,* p. 7.

5. Bieber, *History of the Greek and Roman Theatres,* pp. 20-21.

6. A wealth of scholarship on Greek tragedy has long maintained that poetry and tragedy were, in essence, opposed to philosophy. The structure of this Part obviously challenges that assumption, which is curious even for the reason that both "theatre" and "theory" emanate from the same root verb in Greek. Walter Kaufmann has criticized the Nietzschean view that Socratic philosophy killed tragic theatre, in his *Tragedy and Philosophy.* My contention here is that tragic theatre and philosphy have profound commonalities. However, no one puts it more succinctly than Jaeger, who writes: "it was Aeschylus whom Aristophanes conjured up from the lower world as the only man (in the absence of a Platonic censorship) who could recall poetry to its true function." (*Paideia,* p. 247.)

Games, one of the fighters was hit, and the spectators cried out. But Aeschylus nudged Ion of Chios and said: 'See what training does; the man who was hit keeps silence, the spectators shout.' "[7] Aeschylus was the poet of pithy phrases, of words so sparingly used they conveyed more by omission than could ever be transmitted in vociferous outburst. And he expected the same from his audience. He has Eteocles utter these words, in *Seven Against Thebes*: "Is this for the city's safety, is this enheartening for our beleaguered army, to have you falling at the images of the city's gods crying and howling. . . . Damnation! Can you not endure in silence?" (182-85, 252).[8] For Aeschylus, the act of silence might require more courage than angry speech that altogether paralyzed action.

Athenian audiences at that time were not notorious for this sort of discipline, however. Although Aeschylus was cautious not to bluntly offend his fellow citizens after the penalties inflicted upon his colleague, Phyrnicus, he was never solicitous. No tragedian made more discreet use of his teaching powers than did Aeschylus, for whom this vocation was the supreme civic obligation. Hired by the city, he was responsible to its citizens, was judged by them, and attempted through the theatre to educate them for the task of judgment. The nature of that education will be clearer once we have examined the principal dramatic conception in his extant tragedies, that of the ruler and leadership.

It is essential in reading Aeschylus that one concentrate on the particular relations between premeditation, the act itself, and the realizations that ensue upon action. In this way, the act is always a lesson. All of Aeschylus' plays,

7. Quoted in William B. Stanford, *Aeschylus in his Style: A Study in Language and Personality,* p. 132.

8. All quotations from the tragedies of Aeschylus are taken from *The Complete Greek Tragedies,* ed. D. Grene and R. Lattimore, Vol. I, unless otherwise stated; line numbers are indicated in text, in parentheses.

except for *Prometheus Bound* (which is reserved for final and special investigation), center upon the *decision to act* taken by the ruler, a decision sometimes taken with the participation of his people but always impinging upon their collective destiny. For the most part, the action itself is strangely secondary to the elements composing the conscious decision to act. The audience already knows the outcome, of course, and the manner in which the heroic ruler or leader confronts his ultimate action claims the entire dramatic performance. A focus upon the nature of rulership, in this sense, emanates directly from Aeschylus' dramatic treatment of the constructive *and* detrimental possibilities of political action.

We find a variety of rulers in Aeschylus' work, primarily monarchs: from *The Persians,* Xerxes the military despot; from *Seven Against Thebes,* Eteocles the soldier-King; from *The Suppliants,* Pelasgus the constitutional monarch; and in the *Oresteia,* king and queen, a prince and judges.[9] When considered from a chronological perspective, a pattern somewhat like the following emerges: *The Persians* (472) and *Seven Against Thebes* (467) depict the ruler in war; *The Suppliants* (463) and the *Oresteia* (458) give us the ruler under law; and eventually in *Prometheus Bound* (456) we have the first theoretical dialogue on the just ruler.

War and law dominate the Aeschylean tragic universe, because building upon the visions of Solon and Heraclitus, he regards the city as, by nature, contradictory. From its very creation, the city is designed for defensive combat and survives or is destroyed by the subsequent utilization of military power.[10] Equally, the city marks the beginning of law as the measure of human action, founded upon the substitution of restrained deliberation in public institutions

9. There is a similar typology suggested in Virginia Woods Callahan, "Types of Rulers in the Plays of Aeschylus."

10. G. Glotz agrees with Coulanges, in discussing the origin of the city, that "self-defense was its first necessity," *The Greek City and Its Institutions,* p. 18.

for clan bloodshed. However, war confounds the tribunals in a temporary suspension of law, as the instruments of polity become the instruments of sheer violence. There is no permanent formulation for this coexistence of war and law in the city-state's political form; and its very irresoluteness is the reason the city's potential for justice depends upon the comprehension and foresight of the ruler who must meet each new political situation. A conflagration might either fragment his city or unify it against a common external danger. Likewise, the ruler can attend to the exigencies of war as he defends his own shores, or he can initiate war as a form of aggressive policy. These differences are extremely critical for Aeschylus, who like Heraclitus believed war to be the perpetual star of the political constellation and nevertheless longed for the just polity. One writer has said of Heraclitus what could readily be ascribed to Aeschylus: "La vision politique d'Héraclite est tragique, comme est toute sa pensée. Elle s'attache à montrer aux hommes les liens qui les tiennent. La cité est ce qui englobe la guerre, la justice et la loi; la loi—et encore plus la justice—est ce qui doit englober la guerre et la cité . . . la vision de l'unité des contraires . . . est fondamentale."[11] Aeschylus works with this theme—the unity of opposites—most poignantly in his first extant composition, *The Persians*.

From many vantage points *The Persians* is a shocking play and commends the political maturity of Athenians at that time, who were willing not only to view it but to adorn it with a first prize. If it merely concerned the highest moment of Athenian military courage and honor, the unexpected defeat of the imperialist Persians, it would have been consigned to the more banal and undistinguished self-congratulatory works, like American anti-Nazi films of the 1940s. Aeschylus, though, sets *The Persians*

11. Kostas Axelos, *Héraclite et la philosophie,* p. 159.

not in the land of victory but in the land of defeat, entreating his audience to acknowledge the magnificence of that defeated country and, beyond this, to recognize that the repulsion of the Persians was owing to more than their own men's bravery. Athenians in the audience "had almost to forget who they were and to concentrate on the common humanity which they shared with their former enemy."[12]

The Persians is a study of comparative leadership during war. The leader who fails and brings destruction to his own army, which had been "Fearful in aspect, Dreadful in battle" (27-28), is Xerxes. The leader with whom Xerxes is compared is never once mentioned in the play, although every Athenian would have whispered the name, Themistocles. What manner of man Xerxes is appears most in contrast to his father, Darius, who had led Persia to legendary conquests. Darius is called the "mild, unconquerable king" (856) who gave Persians "a great and good life . . . Civilly ordered" (853-54), whereas his son Xerxes is characterized as "young in age as sense" (782-83). The distressed ghost Darius is made to wonder: "Had not my son diseased his sense?" (750). Son apart from father in these lines, Athenians would be compelled beyond their inclination to enrich the habitually poor perception of an enemy. Persia was not undone because it lacked the Athenian democratic form of government, or because it was an unmitigated despotism. To the contrary, Aeschylus was demonstrating the potential fate of *any* political order, should it acquire certain kinds of leaders.

Xerxes exemplifies the most regrettable political rulership Aeschylus can portray, with the exceptions of Clytaemestra in the *Oresteia* and Zeus in *Prometheus Bound*. He is vain, "by folly thought to conquer all the gods" (749). He ignores wise precedent and counsel in word and example, and thus brings the divine as well as human wrath upon

12. Podlecki, *Political Background*, p. 8.

himself and his people. For, as has been asserted, the divine sphere is ever attuned to the human in Aeschylean tragedy; Darius says of the great leader, Cyrus, "No god resented him, for he was wise" (772).[13] In order to comprehend the political extravagance of Xerxes' mistakes, one must recollect how unusual was the empire that fell vanquished by his shortsighted strategies. Whatever historical inadequacies of the Aeschylean depiction of Darius, he did by other accounts show considerable respect for Persia's holdings in Egypt, having preserved Egyptian tradition and religion. He made efforts "to link Egypt to the rest of his empire and to the Mediterranean world. . . . He kept Naucratis open to Greek traders, most of whom now came from Athens."[14] This was a tremendous service to an Attica highly dependent upon foreign trade because of its poor stock in metals, deforestation at an early date, and mediocre soil in most parts of its land.[15] If we keep in mind that Egypt and Greece were Persia's regional competitors for power, Darius' rulership attests to a certain flexibility of governance and especially to an avoidance of total domination as a governing policy. Persia was a wealthy colonial power, but as Rostovtzeff tells us: "Royal riches do not necessarily imply the well-being of subjects. But the ever-increasing prosperity, in Persian times, of the Phoenician cities, of the Caravan cities of Syria and Mesopotamia, and of Babylon is evidence that the wealth of the rulers was based upon the wealth of their subjects. It should be noticed that most of the satrapies of Persia, other than Egypt, Asia Minor enjoyed a lasting peace for at least three

13. E. R. Dodds writes that the Greeks before Plato believed gods were "not timeless beings external to the cosmos; they are part of its furniture. . . . In the conception of such beings there was nothing to exclude the assumption of a moral development." *The Ancient Concept of Progress*, p. 42.

14. M. Rostovtzeff, *The Social and Economic History of the Hellenistic World*, Vol. 1, p. 82.

15. *Ibid.*, p. 91.

centuries, a rare phenomenon in the history of the ancient world."[16]

Aeschylus' Darius in the *Persians* is obviously meant to bring this point home, and Xerxes' vastly differing portrait is the key to all Aeschylus has to say about the power of a leader to alter the political character of his state. Aeschylus introduces in this play the possibility of polluting the city by one's actions or policies, particularly military policies. We have the first glimpse of what E. R. Dodds has called the cause of Greece's destruction at the end of the fifth century: "systematic irrationality." Aeschylus introduces this notion in the form of an analogy, which will later be epitomized in Plato's *Republic*. As the psyche's forces are to the individual, so are individuals to the city. "The city is man writ large," and some men can fortify the city just as wisdom, if it is in command, fortifies the soul, while others, as blind passion rends the soul, impel the city to its own disintegration—"As it were, a sea drives on the wave" (*Seven Against Thebes* 758-59). A ruler can alter a city's identity just as the psyche's forces can determine the character of an individual; the ruler's character *is* the city's destiny. It was so with Persia.

Aeschylus illustrates that only the worst of leaders can descend from great achievements in so short a time. Xerxes, in his frenzy for immediate military victory over Athens, swept the whole of Persia to desolation. The lamentation for Xerxes at the end of the play reveals this: Persia's fate is consummately bound to the prideful mistakes of its young leader. When Xerxes speaks the words, "pity the host" (1062), he identifies his own pain with that of the city: "Through the city [runs] lamentation," and the Chorus echoes, "O Persian land in hardness stepped" (1071, 1074). Persia at the close of the play shares the tragic predicament of its host, a crystallization which Thucydides,

16. *Ibid.*, p. 83.

influenced by Aeschylus, will bring to its full conclusion in his *History of the Peloponnesian War*.[17]

Although Aeschylus is not so much focusing on Athens' triumph as upon the reason for Persia's downfall, he does credit Themistocles with decisive leadership on Athen's behalf. We learn this from the fact that Aeschylus keeps before us constantly the battle at Salamis, which had been the strategic turning point in the war for the Athenians.[18] Aeschylus fought in this remarkable battle under the command of Themistocles, who masterminded it as well as the course of the entire conflict.[19] At the time *The Persians* was produced, Themistocles had already found himself on the short end of personal contests for power among the ruling elites of Athens, and probably betrayed by jealous colleagues. No Athenian audience could possibly view *The Persians* without feeling shame, at the memory of his noble leadership under fire, having now so rapidly disavowed him. They, too, would remember him as the architect of Athens' new centrality and prominence in the Greek world; and this Aeschylus would put before them again, in *Seven Against Thebes* and in *The Suppliants*.

What was it that Aeschylus so admired in Themistocles and feared that his people were losing in his underserved exile? Unlike his foe Xerxes, Themistocles was not vain even at the moment of success. Herodotus quotes Themistocles: "It is not I who have accomplished this, but the gods and heroes who grudged one man to be king of Asia and Europe . . . who treated sacred and private dwellings in the same way, burning and overturning the gods' images."[20]

17. See Cornford, *Thucydides Mythhistoricus*, p. 182, for an excellent discussion of the Melian Dialogue as a special form of madness: "blindness and insolence."

18. Podlecki, *Political Background*, p. 12. Aeschylus' great admiration for Themistocles and his later problems with Pericles are treated in Podlecki's analysis.

19. See Herman Bengtson, ed. (Conway, tr.), *The Greeks and the Persians, From the Sixth to the Fourth Centuries*.

20. Quoted in Podlecki, *Political Background*, p. 23.

Aeschylus much prefigures this description in *The Persians* (809-12). Themistocles was free of corrosive pressures as well; his Athenian supporters came mainly from the poor and underprivileged, as opposed to the middle-class merchants and rich landowners.[21] He held a long-range political vision for all of Greece, even before the Persian conflict, seeking an internally fortified Peloponnese of voluntary memberships to offset an attack such as that sustained by Miletus. But, "like so many of his other policies—Themistocles' advances to Ionia, his support of the Ionian revolt and his attempts to dislodge the Ionians before Salamis— were brought to fruition only by his successors," and not in terms of his long-range policy.[22]

Themistocles' foresight in politics amounted to a radically different conception of the political unit than had ever been conceived in the world of empires, cities, villages, and vast nomadic stretches. He envisioned the spirit of city loyalty—or in the contemporary world, nationalism—as autonomous and at the same time as part of a greater cooperation in the whole of Greece. This was a possible answer to the devastation of internecine conflict that accompanied the construction of separate and autonomous political units: the city or nation that would both build its own walls, secure its own laws and identity, and yet contribute beyond itself to achieving a union capable of dismantling internal power struggles and rebuffing external ones. Aeschylus suspected that Themistocles' attempts at constructing a regional political organization to avoid major wars would not serve as a principle to his fellow Athenians. By the end of his life, in 456, he knew not only the realization of this fear, but of one worse: the pursuit of war for its own sake.

If we may abbreviate the qualities Aeschylus admired in Darius and the leader at Salamis to foresight, intelligence,

21. C. M. Bowra, *Periclean Athens*, p. 22.
22. Podlecki, *Political Background*, p. 21.

and modesty, we find these qualities reappearing in Eteocles of *Seven Against Thebes* but within a different setting. The problem posed by the Oedipus myth in this play is not resolved until the *Eumenides*, some nine years later. Aeschylus had to confront the issue of sons suffering for the sins of their fathers, given his predilection for a special breed of leadership. Indeed, if the right sort of ruler is at the head of state but was born into a situation of irreversible ancient curse, what good is his insight, his plan, his courage? Aeschylus, here and elsewhere, attempts to deny the ultimate *ruling* force of the "Erinyes" in the human psyche and in political governance. The solution dramatized in the *Eumenides* is that only an obliteration of clan retribution (the curse of the Erinyes) through the establishment of a disinterested public institution can liberate responsible leadership from ancient curse, by providing the privilege of objective judgment, particularly in cases of murder.

In *Seven Against Thebes* there is no resolution of the dilemma "who shall wash away the stain?" (739), though something more tragic, more tenuous than resolution is enacted: the limitations of even good leadership, the dependence of the ruler in crisis upon the courage and awareness of those he rules. The leader and his city exist in a sort of fluid partnership; one can never abandon completely to the other the tasks of governance, especially within a democracy. The tension between self and community is at a high pitch in this drama. Thus, we discover Aeschylus' Eteocles summarily dismissing his female chorus when it bewails the imminent threat to the city. Chorus: "Fellow-citizen Gods, grant me not to be a slave." Eteocles: "It is you who enslave yourselves, and all the city" (253-54). The external offender may not harm the city more than the errant citizen whose complaints exclude the possibilities of collective action. That had been the lesson of the Persian wars.

As invaders approach the city's gates, Eteocles must

somehow, against each avenue of blindness and despair, make his people *see* their situation in its totality, see themselves as a whole beyond their separate grief, just as Aeschylus would have his audience see Thebes in the totality of its plight. The notion of standing one's ground honorably, under seige, is once again a tribute to Themistocles. It was he who had sponsored the fortification of Athens and supervised the construction of the south wall; at the time *Seven Against Thebes* was produced, the issue of internal reinforcement in Athens was again controversial. One of Aeschylus' dramatic purposes must have been to champion his former commander's policy in this tragedy on Thebes.[23] Aeschylus portrays in the *Seven* the peculiar passion of cleaving to one's native land, the age-old insistence upon independence from political claims based purely on superior might, a passion which Athens will eventually detest when it is met at the Island of Melos.

Seven Against Thebes teaches us that war is sometimes necessary, and that its price is always too high: a periodic malady during which the best men will be lost. It is obviously not to be initiated as a foreign policy, for beyond the human cost, the gods will deal unmercifully with those who begin a wrong-doing. Aeschylus places before the Athenian audience the awesome task of judging rulers in a context of war. Never urging them to sightless patriotism, he regards bravery in defense of one's land a virtue. But only a crazed and bestial country would seek out war; the surest protection of national power is not a policy of domination but a just government. In the Aeschylean universe, a city that has not suffered internal pollution is assured of victory in the long run. Mr. Keynes, had he found himself in fifth-century Athens, would have to reconsider his maxim: in the long run we are all part of some political order of which human death is merely punctuation. Eco-

---

23. Supported in *ibid.*, p. 41.

nomic stability may be a limited policy of the short run, but the justice of an entire society can only be dealt with in a total theoretical vision.

After *Seven Against Thebes* the city of Athens, with its customary indifference to its best teachers, seemed, in retrospect, to have moved steadily toward the war that would prove suicidal. And Aeschylus, as if in defiance, concentrated his tragedies more and more upon internal political justice, and less directly upon the problem of war. Attentive to the policies of his contemporary Athens, he tries to educate his audience for a constructive political future with all the powers of the theatre available to him: the visibility of past precedent, "ruth" for human suffering, and the projection of an ideal conception of justice.[24] Within the context of polis and tragic theatre, the relationship between the rulers and Aeschylus would have a decisive impact upon his progress in this objective. Aeschylus' relationship with Pericles began amicably in 472, when Pericles was choregus for *The Persians*,[25] but within a decade they would have made an unlikely pair as openly critical references to Periclean policies appear in the *Oresteia*. If Aeschylus does find himself at odds with Pericles, it must have to do with Pericles' eager departure from the Themistoclean project of unifying Greece in favor of an imperialistic foreign policy. We shall return to this point in our discussion of *Prometheus Bound*.

Aeschylus had shown his audience what he expected of leadership in face of violent conflict. In *The Suppliants*, he turns to the responsibilities of a constitutional monarchy, and we have the first dramatization in theatre of the ruler hesitating to act before two disagreeable alternatives. Either King Pelasgus admits the suppliant maidens into

24. Walter Kaufmann offers an important analysis of the notion of "ruth" in *Tragedy and Philosophy*.

25. Podlecki, *Political Background*, p. 34.

Argos for protection from their Egyptian pursuers, or he denies them access to his city of Argos, turning away "a needy stranger" (202). The maidens wonder if the King will "be compassionate, defend us with care" (216) once he knows they have chosen voluntary exile from a forced marriage to their father's enemies. If Pelasgus denies the maidens shelter, he will prove unyielding (a quality Aeschylus will immortalize in *Prometheus'* Zeus) and inhospitable to those less fortunate beyond his city's walls. Yet, if he accedes to the maidens' request, he risks war in his peaceful city, for the Egyptian pursuers will hardly take Argive interference lightly. Should he involve his city in the misfortune of others?

A theme reappears here that is incorporated into *The Persians* and which we again associate with Themistocles: whether a city can be entirely self-interested and still be just; whether a polity can afford the luxury of isolation and rigidity vis-à-vis other polities without ultimately turning that inflexibility in an ingrown manner upon its own people, losing compassion and loosening a madness from the depths of its own power.[26] The question Aeschylus puts to Pelasgus is whether his city can be *open* to the outside world without becoming aggressive toward it; a middle course, infrequently observed by great powers, between insularity and imperialism.

Could one believe this torment to be the words of an Aeschylean king?

> Pollution on my enemies! Without
> Harm I cannot aid you; nor is it sensible
> to despise these your earnest prayers.
> I am at a loss, and fearful is my heart.
> To act or not to act and choose success.
>
> (376-80)

---

26. See Plato, *Laws*, 951.

We are more assured it is Pelasgus when the good King
states the nature of his responsibility:

> The choice is not easy: choose me not as judge.
> I said before that never would I act
> Alone, apart from the people, though I am ruler;
> So never may people say, if evil comes,
> Respecting aliens the city you destroyed.
>
> (397-401)

Pelasgus will judge and then act only with his entire city or
not at all. In this decision, Aeschylus exalts, for Athenians,
the political obligation of a democracy: that it remain the
final tragic agent in its own destiny. Aeschylus regarded
Argos as such a democracy, and his tribute to this city had a
contemporary end in view. At the time of *The Suppliants*,
the alliance of Athens with Argos was proposed by the
radicals against the conservative position under Cimon
that preserved the old isolationist ties to Sparta. The
Argive alliance had been a Themistoclean objective, and it
finally won acceptance by the year 460, possibly with the
dramatic assistance of Aeschylus' *Suppliants*.[27] Aeschylus
was thinking of Argive hospitality to Themistocles after his
rude ostracism by Athens, in the vivid characterization of
the suppliant maidens, intending, of course, to remind
Athenians of their unattractive similarity to the pursuers.[28]

Aeschylus' last effort, while still in Athens, to nourish the
political perception of his fellow citizens represents perhaps the finest tragedy ever written, the *Oresteia*. This
trilogy, composed in 458, when the author had but three
years to live, contains his most exquisite poetry and engulfs

27. Podlecki, *Political Background,* p. 60.
28. *Ibid.,* p. 166. Podlecki quotes F. Stoessl, "Aeschylus as a Political Thinker,"
AJP (1952), pp. 125-26: "There can be no doubt that Aeschylus' Danaids trilogy,
which testifies to such great and warm sympathy for the democratic state in the
Peloponnese likewise must have worked in the direction of a rapprochement with
Argos. Aeschylus has in any case approved of Themistocles' foreign policy and
supported it by his means, those of tragic poetry."

us in the full political and spiritual journey of all his tragic dramas. The import of an entire life's vision has rarely ever been so perfectly incarnated in a single work of art. From Agamemnon's appalling execution at the hands of his own wife, in the first play, to the acquittal of Orestes for his own violent act, in the last play, an indomitable tragedian strives to prevent forever the domination of the Erinyes in the proceedings of public and collective life. Dodds captures the significance of Orestes' development in this trilogy by distinguishing his act from that of his mother, Clytaemestra: "He is aware that his act is a crime, even before he has committed it . . . but receiving it as a duty, he stands as a type of all those who take upon themselves the 'necessary guilt of human action.' Orestes has not merely suffered his situation, he has understood it, and in a sense mastered it; it is his *mathos* which makes him worthy of salvation."[29]

The tragic rhythm of this trilogy is that of all Aeschylean theatre. It soars outward to embrace historical precedent: has Persia overstepped itself?, his theatre had demanded. And with the answer comes an astonishing willingness to act constructively where others have demonstrated the futility of certain actions. Yet, there is an undercurrent to this positive conception of human action that reflects his sense of man's equally strong capacity for self-destruction, and that forms a permanent chorus on the Aeschylean stage. Jaeger describes this for us as Aeschylus' "faith in the perfect and uninterrupted justice of God's government of the world, and his horrified realization of the daemonic cruelty and perfidiousness of *até*, which leads man to violate the world-order and inevitably to be punished for his violation."[30] His tragic resolution at the conclusion of the *Eumenides* is meant to impress Athenians with the unique quality of civic institutions, such as the Areopagus

29. E. R. Dodds, *The Ancient Concept of Progress,* p. 61.
30. Jaeger, *Paideia,* pp. 258-9.

Court, within which "even the bitterest feud can and should end in reconcilation."[31]

Contentious discord was the hallmark of this transitional period in Athenian history. Just prior to Pericles' assumption of power, Ephialtes had been assassinated, probably by a conservative enclave opposed to his transfer of specific jurisdictional authority from the old Areopagus to the Boule and the ecclesia.[32] There was a mounting fear of civil war during the years 460-458, and recent evidence documents substantial losses incurred by Athenian armies involved in foreign conflicts.[33] Athenian theatre audiences at this time must have been sensitive to the sharp contrast of the current political atmosphere as compared to their perception of it a mere twelve years before, when they had viewed *The Persians* with the blush of victory still in their cheeks.

It is in the *Eumenides* of the *Oresteia* that one discovers Aeschylus growing wary of what was becoming the one-man rule of Pericles. The *Eumenides* is the only Aeschylean play in which there is no king, and characteristically it casts more light upon the nature of kingship for this reason. The tragic theatre itself, aiming at the invisible social reality, always reveals the political order within which it resides by offering it the counter-example, the otherness that any society is too self-centered to grasp. Impartiality was also a singular benefit of the Areopagus, and it is precisely in reaction to Pericles' tampering with specific Court traditions that Aeschylus exposes him to subtle censure in this play. The Areopagus was to be recalled in awe and respect when Athene speaks: "I shall select judges of manslaughter, and swear them in, establish a court into all time to

31. E. R. Dodds, *The Ancient Concept of Progress*, p. 52.

32. P. J. Rhodes explains Ephialtes' reforms as completing the previous Cleisthenes' democratization of the Boule and not as a dismantlement of the Areopagus as such, in *The Athenian Boule*, p. 223.

33. E. R. Dodds notes this in *The Ancient Concept of Progress*, p. 52.

come. . . . I will pick the finest of my citizens, and come back. They shall swear to make no judgment that is not just, And make clear where in this action the truth lies" (483-84, 487-89).

Aristotle's *Constitution of Athens* informs us the first Areopagus was to "maintain" the laws, Solon having later assigned to it the function of "nomophylakia" or overseer.[34] In this capacity, it was to retain an imposing authority over legislative, judicial, and educational matters. It was to have the best men, and above all the jurymen would not be tempted by financial gain. By the year the *Eumenides* was performed, however, Pericles had instituted pay for jury members, and, as Podlecki persuasively argues, he had removed the major function of overseer from the Areopagus to a small council responsible to himself.[35] Two passages in the *Eumenides* declare Aeschylus' evident displeasure regarding the Periclean innovations. First, the goddess of wisdom warns against meddling with laws: "all while the people do not muddy their own laws with foul infusions. But if bright water you stain with mud, you nevermore will find it fit to drink" (693-95). And soon thereafter, Athene adds: "I establish this tribunal, It shall be untouched by money-making, grave but quick to wrath, watchful to protect those who sleep, a sentry on the land" (704-6). These lines would have constituted an obvious affront to Pericles.

There is a hint, especially in the last two lines quoted above, of what is possibly uppermost in Aeschylus' mind. The Court is designed to watch, to protect, and to rise in anger, and one cannot but wonder whether he is urging the preservation of these capacities at this time because there was something to be ever watchful for: the tyrannical proclivities of even a distinguished democratic polis. This sense of tyranny encompassed a power too concentrated in

34. Podlecki, *Political Background,* p. 96.
35. *Ibid.,* p. 97.

one man, a political policy too incremental to admit of any foresight, a city too consumed in its own quotidian interests. In addition, it is as if the debasement of the Areopagus signals a potential dismantlement of yet another institution, though in different ways, that institution being his own tragic theatre. For a leader who felt constrained by Court decisions that might hinder his expansionist schemes was certain to resent an art form that subverted them in the full light of day. Given his probable disillusionment as an educator trying to turn Athenians toward the international policies of Themistocles and away from short-run national interest, Aeschylus may have believed the only institution that could continue to educate and to provide an open forum long after the theatre might have been eclipsed would be the Court, and that its restoration as an "overseer" was fundamental. This is why Athene's dialogue is primarily centered on the nature of the Areopagus as it was *before* Pericles altered it.

If it is true that Aeschylus perceived the Court, like the theatre, to be a source of political education, then the direction of his vocation as tragedian parallels Plato's development in political philosophy. After having written his major dialogue on the city and justice at the beginning of his career, Plato turned to the *Laws* at the end of his life, perhaps like Aeschylus, hoping to salvage something of his original vision in the murky labyrinth of the legal process, short of the realization of his Republic. However, neither Aeschylus nor Plato would ever have embraced law as a surrogate for human wisdom, and therefore this excursion is basically tragic for them both (as it would not be for Hobbes, for example). The very meaning of law and its tragic aspect resided in its human use.[36]

The meaning of political education in relation to the

36. Plato, *Laws*, 875. R. Kuhns writes: "The view that tragedy is a serious representation of matters pertaining to justice in the city is held by both Aeschylus and Plato" (*The House, the City, and the Judge*, p. 65).

theatre is nowhere better illuminated than in the *Oresteia*. Just as the theatre begins as an art form within the developing context of the polis, its subject matter continues to reflect fundamentally political needs and dilemmas. In a contemporary framework, where politics and the public itself have in many nations been reduced to arenas of private competing interests, theatre that is political is thought to be the shoddy equivalent of proselytism and pamphleteering. Of course, nothing could be further from the original meaning of "political," which expresses the whole of collective life in the polis. And the theatre that was, and still is, profoundly political is such at the core of its very dramatic purposes, and because its audience exists as a polity. This does not mean the theatre was, in any remote sense, ideological.

Aeschylean tragedy addresses itself continually to Athenian political controversies of the day, but no ideological position emerges from almost fifty years of tragic presentations. In 460, Aeschylus' *The Suppliants* lent support to liberals against conservatives in a dispute over alliance with Argos or Sparta. In 458, in the *Eumenides*, we find Aeschylus criticizing Periclean "radical" reforms, and seeming to adopt a more conservative outlook. But Aeschylus was not concerned with the relative significance of ideological labels, which have all the permanence of fashion. He was devoted to the well-being of Athens, the city; and as he saw it, no special interest within that city could act more constructively over the long term than a disinterested public institution that would secure the least parochial and broadest possible spectrum of political alternatives. This meant, at best, choosing the Themistoclean maxim of international stability as the priority in defining national interest. To see one's city as part of a larger configuration of power struggles, however, is an insight most cities or nations have appreciated only in eulogy. At the very least, this meant that citizen-juries would not be tainted by the confusion of profit with justice.

The *Eumenides* notes Aeschylus' disparagement of jury pay, but it does not touch upon the earlier reforms of the Areopagus by Ephialtes, or even Cleisthenes. For it was not that Aeschylus objected to democratization as such—*The Suppliants* and *Prometheus Bound* passionately argue the reverse—but that certain democratic measures defiled the public interest. He reserved negative judgment only for the latter. Similarly, P. J. Rhodes has written with respect to this judgment: "it should not have been necessary to introduce a salary in war time for an office which conferred exemption from military service on the holder."[37] Another historian has these reservations to add to a critique of the Periclean innovations:

> Pericles' introduction of the *diaitai* (pay for jurymen) was in some respects, however, a benefit of dubious, even questionable nature. . . . Although the state paid them only enough for a minimum subsistence, there were nevertheless a great number of recipients of these state funds, and thus the spirit in which these sums were accepted, as well as the actual amount of the sums, became a factor in the political situation . . . the measure introduced by Pericles marked the beginning of a downward path that was to be followed much further by Cleon and other demagogues.[38]

Thus it would appear there was little for which to commend Pericles at that time, and it could not have been the vocation of tragic theatre to remain indifferent to policies that would prove harmful to the whole community. For Aeschylus, the theatre and the Court served Athens in the same way Tocqueville would later say the free press served American democracy: as the democratic instruments of liberty par excellence.

37. P. J. Rhodes, *The Athenian Boule*, pp. 13-14.
38. H. Bengtson (ed.), *The Greeks and the Persians*, p. 89.

Hope and determination do overtake the theatre audience in the closing lines of the *Eumenides,* and it is significant that Athene always speaks on behalf of the Aeropagus, because in the absence of new rulership this confidence in the future belongs to the Court:

CHORUS: Life will give you no regrets.

ATHENE: Well said. I assent to all the burden of your prayers. . . . Flower of all the land of Theseus, let them issue now, grave companies, maidens, wives, elder women, in processional . . . so that the kindly company of these within our ground may share in the future of strong men to come.

(1020-21, 1025-31)

4. Theatre of Political Memory

I understand, said Glaucon: You mean this common-
wealth we have been founding in the realm of discourse;
for I think it nowhere exists on earth.

No, I replied; but perhaps there is a pattern set up in
the heavens for one who desires to see it and, seeing it, to
found one in himself. But whether it exists anywhere or
ever will exist is no matter; for this is the only common-
wealth in whose politics he can ever take part.

Plato, *Republic*

One of the more perplexing passages in the *Republic,*
quoted above, echoes the sort of exclusion always looming
on the Aeschylean stage. The city may not enact the tragedian's vision of political life, but that vision remains
intact symbolizing the only sense of life accessible to human
involvement and identity. The reality of art and the reality
of life are interdependent; and the trouble with societies
that are polluted, from Aeschylus' perspective, or unjust,
in Plato's philosophy, is that they abuse their best men, who
must flee and take refuge like Plato's man in the dust storm.

Fustel de Coulanges has described in his *Ancient City* the
unspeakable loss one experienced in being driven from the
native polis. It was to forfeit air and water, to become a
malevolent spirit people would shun from their domains; it
was to gain a fearful desert and to lose one's own soul.
Socrates could not consider it, preferring death. Yet, after
458 Aeschylus finds himself in Sicily, never to return to
Athens and his theatre for tragedy. Why he has left his city
and why he is composing his final tragedy on foreign soil,
we may never know. But what is palpably evident, and what

perhaps tells a story of its own, is the inescapable contrast between the last promising lines of the *Oresteia* and these that open *Prometheus Bound*, spoken by Power (κρατοσ): "This is the world's limit that we have come to; this is the Scythian country, an untrodden desolation." By the time Aeschylus composed these lines, classical Athens was at the middle of her life, and he was at the end of his. He would not be present when Athens would lie in the ashes of the Peloponnesian War and the calamity of which *Prometheus Bound* warns would have materialized on the awesome stage of historical reality.

Beyond its startling first act, the entire action of *Prometheus Bound* is distinct from other Aeschylean dramas in being essentially complete before the play commences. There is no major decision to which one leads or from which one backs off. We are presented with an Aeschylean tragedy that is more theoretical than ever before and more transfixed in dialogue. The play is in fact a series of conversations, in which the subjects of defiance and punishment are related to conceptions of justice in the political order. It is, in short, a forerunner of the Platonic dialogue, and this will be illustrated in a comparison of the beginning of *Prometheus* and the opening discussion of justice in the *Republic*.

Prometheus Bound will remain contemporary as long as, in Mao Tse-tung's phrase, men dare to rebel. A god who violates the rules of his cosmic order permanently alters the scope of its power. Against a general injunction by Zeus, Prometheus has given men fire. Zeus is inconsolable in face of this transgression, because fire is the secret of terrestrial powers and, as we learn of Zeus from Prometheus, for the "unhappy breed of mankind he gave no heed, intending to blot the race out and create a new" (233-34). Zeus' perception of men is not in the tragic mode. Assured that they cannot be entrusted with diverse powers, he feels they deserve to perish. Once in conflict with the perception of

Prometheus, however, the two become tragic, for Zeus must deal with human proclivities whether or not he wishes it. We have in this unwonted confrontation the same Aeschylus of the *Persians*, more embittered and more sullen, but with conviction holding to his fundamental tragic belief: men can and must learn to use their powers wisely and justly. The question that unfolds in the tragedy of *Prometheus Bound* is: what is political power like without foresight, compassion, and appeal against "private laws"? The twentieth century is replete with corresponding examples.

As *Prometheus Bound* begins, the official version of justice is enacted by the figures of Power and violence, who chain Prometheus to the rock.[1] They are situated in a "bare and desolate crag in the Caucasus," apart from any cosmic or human order, and there is nothing to endow their action with meaning except the persuasion of what they have to say. Power proclaims that Prometheus requires punishment, "that he may learn to endure and like the sovereignty of Zeus and quit his man-loving disposition" (10-11). Power is the tireless opponent of dissent, the state prosecutor whose surest measure of character is blind conformity. A similar formulation appears in Chapter II of the *Republic*, where Simonides is arguing that justice is "rendering services or injuries to friends or enemies."[2] Socrates, who opposes this widely held Athenian opinion, pleads on the same grounds as does Hephaestus, the ironmaker in *Prometheus* who must carry out Zeus' command and nail "the rascal" to the rock. Hephaestus protests, "I have not the heart to bind violently a God who is my kin here on this wintry cliff" (14-15). To Power, who scorns him for his "pitying in vain," Hephaestus responds: "You are always pitiless, always full of ruthlessness" (42). Is this the agent of

1. Violence is a "muta persona," and Hannah Arendt has noted that for the Greeks violence did connote the impossibility of speech and its civilizing effects.
2. Quotations from Plato's *Republic* are taken from F. Cornford's translation.

justice, without pity, without restraint? Power adds that "There is nothing without discomfort except the overlordship of the Gods. For only Zeus is free" (49-50). When Hephaestus replies, "I know, I have no answer to this" (51), one must marvel at a rulership that enslaves everything around it, rendering only the ruler free.

Finally, Hephaestus touches upon the central dilemma for himself as executioner, and for us as witnesses: he who will receive the punishment, the infliction of harm, will suffer, and to what end? Can this suffering bear the name of justice? Hephaestus tells us: "No one, save Prometheus, can justly blame me" (63). This anticipates closely the first steps Socrates will pursue with Polemarchus:

Can it really be a just man's business to harm any human being?

Certainly; it is right for him to harm bad men who are his enemies.

But does not harming a horse or a dog mean making it a worse horse or dog, so that each will be a less perfect creature in its own special way?

Yes.

Isn't that also true of human beings—that to harm them means making them worse by the standard of human excellence?

Yes.

And is not justice a peculiarly human excellence?

Undoubtedly.

To harm a man, then, must mean making him less just.[3]

Socrates has no sooner shaken the relation of punishment to justice when he must confront the most staggering conception of justice, from Thrasymachus, in Chapter III: "in all states alike 'right' has the same meaning, namely what is for the interest of the party established in power, and that is the strongest. So the sound conclusion is that what is 'right' is the same everywhere: the interest of the

3. *Republic*, I, 334.

stronger party."[4] This is precisely what Power imposes upon the "softhearted" Hephaestus; this is the essence of his act, when at last he turns to Prometheus and exclaims: "Drive the obstinate *jaw of the adamantine wedge* right through his breast; drive it hard. . . . Now, play the insolent; now, plunder the Gods' privileges and give them to creatures of a day. What drop of your sufferings can mortals spare you?" (64-65, 32-83, emphasis added). He introduces the vulgar equation Thrasymachus will later urge upon us: might equals right; merely through superior force, it makes its own law, its own justice. As Hephaestus had warned his ill-fated friend, Prometheus, at the outset: "Always the grievous burden of your torture will be there to wear you down; for he that shall cause it to cease has yet to be born" (25-26). The equation "might is right" does rule in the cosmos of Zeus, but it is not justice, and the proof that it is not is the burden of the play, just as it is the burden of Plato's *Republic*.

Socrates, in order to undermine Thrasymachus' assertion, develops the conception of ruling as an art:

And so every art seeks, not its own advantage—for it has no deficiencies—but the interest of the subject on which it is exercised.

It appears so.

But surely Thrasymachus, every art has authority and superior power over its subject.

To this he agreed, though very reluctantly.

So far as arts are concerned, then, no art ever studies or enjoins the interest of the superior or stronger party, but always that of the weaker over which it has authority. . . .

Thus every art has its own function and benefits its proper subject.[5]

This formulation is the meaning of what Aeschylus has dramatized as Promethean liberation: the emergence of

4. *Republic*, I, 338.
5. *Republic*, I, 342-346.

the ruler's art as power that benefits its subjects.[6] In both
Aeschylus' *Prometheus* and Plato's *Republic*, the tragic and
the political become the ruler's art and the political order in
which it can be best engendered. The difference lies in
Plato's knowledge of a postwar Athens that had lost confidence in the polis for the first time since its formation.
Good leadership was as central for Plato as it had been to
Aeschylus, but it too easily deteriorated into tyranny in the
absence of a specific environment, that of the Republic
devoted to the education of good rulers. Plato did pursue
in terms of philosophy what Aeschylus had tried to project
in tragedy: what constituted the just ruler, and how those
he led could become just and wise.

There is one more similarity between the opening discussions of *Prometheus* and the *Republic*, and this comes in
Chapter Four of the *Republic*, where injustice is deemed "a
source of weakness" because it generates fragmentation
and disunity to poison constructive action.[7] This is a theme
first attributed to the rule of Zeus in *Prometheus*. Prometheus anticipates that Zeus will one day need him, that he
will feel insecure in his rule of force: "Hastily he'll come to
meet my haste, to join in amity and union with me—one
day he shall come" (194-95). A bit later, he adds that Zeus'
tyranny is flawed by apprehension and disharmony: "This
is a sickness rooted and inherent in the nature of a tyranny:
That he that holds it does not trust his friends" (225-27).
Finally, Prometheus will tell his companion in misery, Io,

6. It is enlightening to compare the meaning which the term "Promethean
liberation" has assumed in the following passage from Samuel P. Huntington,
Political Order in Changing Societies, p. 99: "Above all, modernization involves belief
in the capacity of man by reasoned action to change the physical and social
environments. It means the rejection of external restraints on man, the Promethean liberation of man from control by gods, fate and destiny." This is no longer a
tragic conception by the mere removal of some transcendent sense of measure for
political change. And some nations might prefer gods, fate, and destiny to international corporations.

7. *Republic*, I, 351.

that Zeus will fall from power by a weakness rooted in his own mind: "His own witless plans" (762).

Once Prometheus has been sufficiently "hammered" to the rock, Power, Violence, and Hephaestus depart with the latter clearly shattered by the experience. One of the effects of an unjust or tyrannical rule, Aeschylus will portray, is the numbing of sympathy and compassion. In time, force will erase those fragile outward sensitivities men come to feel for one another, sensitivities that can be expressed by the polity between its own members or for those states with which it may come into conflict. But for the leader, Zeus, who rules through pure domination, compassion is expended at the outset, because his rule is also new, unbent by painful precedents. The chorus that precedes Oceanos tells us Zeus' rule is new, composed of "customs that have no law to them" and "what was great before, he brings to nothingness" (150-51). This reminds us of Hephaestus' prior description of Zeus' rule: "For the mind of Zeus is hard to soften with prayer, and every ruler is harsh whose rule is new" (33-34), and of Aeschylus' perpetual judgment of the inexperienced, over-hasty novice at government. From Xerxes to Zeus, it is always a brew for blunder and abuse. The Athenian audience, had it seen *Prometheus,* might have gathered uneasily in the presence of their own new ruler, Pericles, and might have been placed suspiciously before his "inexperienced" political desicions.[8]

Prometheus means "forethinker" and it is certainly the

8. Ehrenberg, *Sophocles and Pericles,* pp. 85-86, relates that Pericles was known in Cratinus' comedies as "Zeus with a peaked head." By 443, Cratinus had depicted him as a tyrannical Zeus expelled by the demos that liberated the Titans. I do not mean to imply, however, that *Prometheus Bound*'s characterization of Zeus is political allegory pure and simple. As E. R. Dodds insists in *The Ancient Concept of Progress,* Aeschylus was not given to this sort of unimaginative political criticism (p. 44). Rather, Zeus represents a certain type of rulership which may have been exemplified by Pericles and others.

quality of foresight alone that Aeschylus retains from the
myth with respect to its appearance in Hesiod, where
Prometheus is no more than a mischevious thief. The first
thing we learn about Prometheus from his own lips is that
he contradicted Zeus for man's sake:

> I gave to mortal man
> a precedence over myself in pity: I can
> win no pity: pitiless is he
> that thus chastises me, a spectacle
> bringing dishonor on the name of Zeus.
>
> (240-44)

To what ends did Prometheus' compassion for man take
him?

> I caused mortals to cease foreseeing doom . . .
> I placed in them blind hopes . . .
> Besides this, I gave them fire . . .
> Yes, and from it they shall learn many crafts.
>
> (250,252,254,256)

Prometheus' sin against Zeus exceeds the gift of fire; he has
taught men that mortality can be the very stuff of an
impulse to create, and that men can begin to use their new
powers beneficially. Thus, the situation represented by
Zeus and Prometheus is one in which political power,
resting in Zeus' anti-humanist hands, is separated from the
long-range Promethean objective that power prove beneficial to human life. Zeus' mindless power is incomplete and
destructive onto itself; Aeschylus urges throughout that
this brute force must be subdued by Prometheus' knowledge in order to salvage the human spirit from utter anni-
hilation.

When Oceanos makes his peculiar entrance, on a sea-
monster, he has "neighborly" advice for Prometheus to
liberate him from his plight. He will speak to Zeus on
Prometheus' behalf if Prometheus will only "give up his
angry mood," mend his ways and shift with the dominant
tide. Oceanos wants Prometheus to plead for foregiveness

and make a gesture toward rapprochement with Zeus. Aeschylus provides Prometheus with wit enough to respond that when his form of knowledge is at the mercy of arbitrary might, discussion is beyond the pale:

OCEANOS: Do you not know, Prometheus, that words are healers of the sick temper?

PROMETHEUS: Yes, if in season due one soothes the heart with them, not tries violently to reduce the swelling anger.

(379-82)

The very fact that Prometheus cannot speak to Zeus, from the nature of his own transgression, is further indication of Zeus' lack of justice as a political ruler. One will recall the excellence of Pelasgus' rule in the *Suppliants* lay in his ability to discuss the dilemma publicly and come to a collective decision with his entire city. But the healing potential of speech wanes in this drama; words are incommensurate to the deeds. Oceanos is eager to be on his way and far from the sight of Prometheus' anger and pain, and Prometheus, knowing he cannot persuade this old "well-intentioned" counsellor, dismisses him: "Off with you, then! Begone! Keep your present mind" (394). As he leaves, his chorus refers again to Zeus with:

This is a tyrant's deed; this is unlovely,
a thing done by a tyrant's private laws,
and with this thing Zeus shows his haughtiness
of temper toward the Gods that were of old.

(402-405)

The words "private laws" could only denote, for Athenians, the bankruptcy of a democratic rule; and by "the Gods of old," Aeschylus might be referring to those men whose principles were the groundwork of the Athenian democracy—Solon and Themistocles. Private laws were synonymous with all that Aeschylus had intrepidly denounced in *Seven Against Thebes* and in the *Oresteia*. Private laws emanated from pre-political, blood-for-blood vengeance that prevented the best men from sustaining their leadership, led to interminable violence, and placed men's acquired knowledge on equal footing with mere chance. There would be no mistaking the meaning of private laws or the accused offender, Zeus.

We are made to understand repeatedly, by the chorus, that Prometheus is being punished because he dared to preserve his own mind in face of Zeus' superior force.

> but I shiver when I see you
> wasted with ten thousand pains,
> all because you did not tremble
> at the name of Zeus; your mind
> was yours, not his, and at its bidding
> you regarded mortal men
> too high, Prometheus.
>
> (540-46)

The chorus describes man as too feeble a subject to be worthy of Prometheus' agony. It is suggested (as will be drawn vividly in Plato's Allegory of the Cave) that man is a prisoner of Zeus' plans. In context, this must mean that man's intelligence is a prisoner of his own blindness and thereby the rule of the mindless stronger:

> You did not see
> the feebleness that draws its breath in gasps,
> a dreamlike feebleness by which the race
> of man is held in bondage, a blind prisoner.
> So the plans of men shall never
> pass the ordered law of Zeus.
>
> (548-53)

The imagery in *Prometheus* is, in general, created and sustained by metaphors of mind and body, with the definite allusion to mind becoming ensnared and obliterated by too violent a body.[9] This imagery attains a melancholy eloquence in the scene of the next visitor, the girl Io. This scene is of special interest as well for the reason that it is not

9. Joseph E. Harry notes that the metaphors dealing with acts and conditions of mind and body in *Prometheus* exceed those in all other Aeschylean plays (*Aeschylus' Prometheus*, p. 46).

Aeschylus' artistic practice to dramatize an encounter between man and woman beyond relationships of family, or masters and servants, or ruler and ruled. But when Io encounters Prometheus, they are not related by any familial, civic, or social ties. They are, rather, victims of a common disaster: opposition to Zeus. We are able to extract a good deal about Zeus' use of power from Io's meeting with Prometheus. The Io legend tells that Zeus has tormented her out of sexual frenzy and then set her upon an endless wandering without family, roots, or purpose of any kind. He has inflicted the same pain upon the girl he desired as he has upon Prometheus, whom he loathes (736-41). Zeus' power produces equal harm whatever his motive, for it always concludes in shortsighted retribution. Io's experience stands as irrefutable proof that Oceanos' methods of currying favor with those in power will be of no avail if that power is a mindless and violent one. Zeus will not treat more gently those he favors. Io is innocent of any "fault" that would merit her "harness of misery" (580); and consistent with tyrannical rule, her suffering is licensed by the ruler's whim.

However, Aeschylus has in his dialectical and tragic view the healing that must attend the abuses of arbitrary power. We discover that Io is to be the bearer both of her own misfortune and of Prometheus' redemption, as one of her descendents will someday free Prometheus from his chains. The surprising element in Prometheus' prophecy is that Zeus himself will be the agent of Io's healing:

> . . . there Zeus shall make you sound of mind
> touching you with a hand that brings no fear,
> and through that touch alone shall come your healing.
> You shall bear Epaphos, dark of skin, his name
> recalling Zeus' touch and his begetting.
>
> (848-52)

The name Epaphos, relating to the circumstances of the child's conception, means "caress" or "gentle touch" but

also "surety," "pledge," "reprisal," and "deliverance."[10]
The imagery called forth by this name is thus manifold and
rich. The power of Zeus will become a "healing might" in a
reconciliation of violence with gentle touch, the implication
being that within Prometheus' perception of Zeus' violent
acts lies the fruit of a new synthesis. When Zeus rescues Io
from degradation, he will exemplify the first compassion
for human misery, and a union of knowledge, humani-
tarian purpose, and power will be in the making.[11] For
once, suffering would teach men not to extend suffering.

Aeschylus reveals in his use of the Io legend that he seeks
a transformation, from within, of the given political universe, rather than coup d'état or civil war. His vision ap-
proximates Marx's theory of socio-historical change, that a
political and economic environment will harbor the seeds
of its own destruction, that its own agents will play a part in
its transformation into a more human society. The characteristics of that environment are also Marxian, for Prometheus insists that the human city and its technology should
benefit all men equally. Io first addresses Prometheus as "O
spirit that has appeared as a common blessing to all men"
(612-13); and Prometheus had informed the chorus pre-
viously that he taught men first to be "masters of their
minds" (443) and then skilled craftsmen: "they did not
know of building houses with bricks to face the sun; they
did not know how to work in wood" (448-49). Prometheus'
gifts were equitably distributed, because he believed diverse technology would prove more humanizing to the
world. Promethean liberation uniquely combines intellectual foresight and philanthropic action; the useful is to be
simultaneously beneficial.[12] But Aeschylus has committed
his protagonist to this resolution—that technology improve
human life—with one absolute provision: the critical rela-

10. Robert Duff Murray, Jr., *The Motif of Io in Aeschylus' Suppliants*, pp. 33-34.
11. *Ibid.*, p. 47.
12. E. A. Havelock, *The Crucifixion of Intellectual Man*, p. 91.

tionship between how power will be used and the necessity
of a *long-range* perspective.

Aeschylus dramatized, in *Prometheus,* his conviction that
a long-term view of governance would, of itself, necessitate
an enlightened governing elite; whereas rulers who are
submerged in short-run goals become absorbed in an
over-concentration upon means rather than upon the
wisdom of the specific goal. Power in the short-term, by
definition, becomes insanely focused on its own exhibition
rather than on its best uses.[13] Moreover, a ruler's long-
range perspective will compel either just action or no action
whatsoever. The ruler who must include so much in his
vision will find it obscured by inevitable uncertainties; he
will be forced to hesitate, and in Hamlet-like fashion, to
have "grounds more relative" for his acts. A ruler's action
should be difficult (as Socrates would later instruct), complicated by the task of governing for the welfare of all his
subjects, and not by the impulse of his own fancy. When a
ruler confines his actions to the short-term, sheer physical
motion begins to overtake his intelligence; his acts descend
to their lowest common denominator, and as Prometheus
describes Zeus, he grows violent in all his ways (733-34).
Havelock has in this context distinguished a class of "primitive society": "the desire to be strong, the identification of
efficiency with speed at the expense of deliberation and
doubt—these, historically speaking, represent the primi-
tivist in man. Societies which exhibit these symptoms are
primitive."[14]

The absence of a long-term view of governance is no
doubt the problem for Aeschylus as he writes *Prometheus*
from Sicily, looking toward an Athens that was pursuing
the limited Periclean objective of a belligerent sea alliance
to launch the Athenian "empire." And one of the reasons

13. Havelock offers a good discussion on this point in *ibid.*, pp. 100-109: "man
must ultimately reconcile his scientific vision with his will to power."
14. *Ibid.*, p. 101.

Prometheus Bound seems to speak to us, across the centuries, is that the distinction between long-range and short-run has finally, in the last decades of the twentieth century, imposed its utmost significance upon the contemporary's world's exhaustible present. Now at last, when time is indeed running out, we should finally become aware that political crises have everything to do with our senses of time. In their day-to-day perceptions of domestic and international conflicts, rulers can often react to onrushing events like the harried subway commuter, who will dive for the door of the 6:15 train at the risk of throwing himself beneath the cars. When political decisions are set in a context of scarce information and the demand for instant decisions, the short run really becomes a fictional time sequence in which there can be little premeditation and certainly no intelligence to inform an action. For Aeschylus, an entire theory of political leadership and order must precede political action. The only time and space dimensions that existed were those of the polis and the character it evinced over its entire history: whether it was noble, generous, compassionate, and self-critical through its public institutions—in other words, whether the city's actions revealed an intelligence. Within the theatre and the city, it would have been nonsense to speak of actions occurring in the "short run"; time made sense only in terms of the whole story.

An aerial reconnaissance over the Greek city-states as they move toward war will show that by the year 434 B.C. they are pursuing suicidal policies of the short run. Each city, unable to see the international configuration of power, will act only in terms of an imminent threat to its own interests. That whole vision of its society which Aeschylean theatre had provided Athens would be gone forever. *Prometheus Bound* is Aeschylus' prophecy that Zeus will fall by his own "witless plans," that a political order in the absence of foresight will crumble on its own poor founda-

tions. Thucydides' *Peloponnesian War* confirms this prophecy, and also documents the more subtle ramifications of
political action mired in the short run.

Thucydides commences with the real cause of the war,
"the one which was formally most kept out of sight": "The
growth of the power of Athens, and the alarm which this
inspired in Lacedaemon, made war inevitable."[15] When
alluding to the cause "most kept out of sight," he must
mean kept out of sight by the Athenians themselves,
because other cities at the mercy of that power had little
difficulty in spotting it. Athenian rulers who wielded that
power, however, kept the futility and potential consequences of their goals out of sight by never taking them
into consideration. Thucydides records the ensuing displacement of ends to means in the near catastrophy of
responding too brutally to the Mitylene Revolt; in the
actual catastrophe at Melos, in the sixteenth year of the
war; and of course in the fatal Sicilian campaign waged by a
city then completely mad.

To Melos, the island loyal to Sparta which preferred to
remain neutral in the conflict, an ally of neither side, the
Athenians replied:

No; for your hostility cannot so much hurt us as your friendship
will be an argument to our subjects of our weakness, and your
enmity of our power.

MELIANS: Is that your subjects' idea of equity, to put those who
have nothing to do with you in the same category with peoples
that are most of them your own colonists, and some conquered
rebels?

ATHENIANS: As far as right goes they think one has as much of it as
the other, and that if any maintain their independence it is
because they are strong, and that if we do not molest them it is
because we are afraid. . . .[16]

15. *The Complete Writings of Thucydides. The Peloponnesian War*, tr. Crawley, Bk. I,
Ch. I.

16. *Ibid.*, Bk. V, Ch. XVII.

By comparing the Athenian speech above with any Aeschylean dialogue composed for Athenian or other great leaders, one can perceive the depths of ruthlessness to which Athens has fallen in a mere forty years. Athenian policy, like that pursued by Zeus in *Prometheus*, can no longer distinguish friends from foes, rebels from neutrals; its fears are for its international "image," and not—like those of Themistocles and Eteocles—for the real defense of their city's grounds, laws, and peace. The desire to be perceived as "strong" while in the process of outright aggression against a people who are peaceful and far inferior in manpower and resources is always cowardly arrogance. Thus Melos, unable to comply, declares to the Athenians, before the latter will slaughter "all the grown men," sell the women and children into slavery, and occupy the island themselves: "to submit is to give ourselves over to despair, while action still preserves for us a hope that we may stand erect."[17]

Thucydides has been called into this discussion of Aeschylean tragedy to show how fundamentally *Prometheus Bound* anticipates the trend of political events in Athens, and particularly how determined Aeschylus is to portray the potential consequences of certain uses of political power. George Thompson has suggested that *Prometheus* terminates in deadlock, that both Zeus and Prometheus are "diseased," and that the play prescribes a cure in terms of their reconciliation.[18] Much is gained from this interpretation; Prometheus, unlike the usual Aeschylean protagonist, is less prudent with speech—a quality which Aeschylus deeply distrusted. The chorus, though sympathetic, says to Prometheus: "You are free of tongue, too free" (182). Prometheus is self-assured in his foresight and intelligence, while Zeus holds power but is mindless and tyrannical. The cure would seem to lie in a synthesis of power and foresight—a combination that will eventually be em-

17. *Ibid.*
18. George Thompson, *Aeschylus, The Prometheus Bound*, p. 11.

bodied in Plato's philosopher-king in the *Republic*. It is evident that Prometheus is given as much dramatic support as he does receive because Aeschylus values his promise more than his faults, and would rather work with him—as Plato will later take on the sophists rather than to abandon the polis to Zeus, Pericles, or Thrasymachus.

By 455 B.C. Aeschylus is dead. How he died is still a matter of conjecture. Judging from various passages in *Prometheus Bound,* he was either well-traveled or had striven through other means to acquire an extensive knowledge of his Mediterranean world. While his own polis, Athens, may have changed since the years of his first tragedies, he had never ceased believing in the Athenian polis of his tragic presentations and in the political order's need for his theatre's vision. The stone engraving at Aeschylus' burial place asks that we remember the tragedian solely for having fought at the battle of Marathon in the Persian Wars. Perhaps he knew that his people would be compelled by this to remember more: that with the battle of Marathon, Athens stood magnificently in charge of her destiny, with neither a history of injustice nor scars from imperial expansion; and that this was the moment in which Aeschylus began to write tragedy, in the fresh morning light of Athens' beginnings as a great city. If we are to understand, then, why theatre disappeared, we must understand as well the passing of that morning into never-ending night.

A discussion of the nature of tragedy comes sooner or later to the moot issue of the "death of tragedy." Walter Kaufmann commits himself rather vaguely to the notion that Aeschylus embodies an anti-tragic optimism about the resolution of tragedy within social institutions, and then adds, without clarification, that tragedy actually dies of despair.[19] Presumably, Sophocles rescues tragedy from Aeschylean optimism, and Euripides extracts its final

19. *Tragedy and Philosophy,* pp. 208-211.

breaths in cynical desolation. What is missing from Kaufmann's treatment, as well as from George Steiner's and others, is that no theory of tragic theatre—which is a peculiarly public art—can possibly be comprehensive without sufficient inquiry into its accompanying political form. For we may legitimately begin to wonder, if tragedy dies of despair, why not music or painting, why not sculpture or dance? Tragedy is unique in that it perishes from the same condition of which its city perishes—the progressive inability to comprehend and direct freedom of action. The unadorned and overwhelming portrayal of political action in Aeschylean theatre proves ultimately too burdensome for Athenian rulers and audience. For a while they are enthralled in the religious beauty and apolitical certainty of Sophoclean tragedy.[20] Then, eventually, they become too absorbed in self-saturation in Euripidean drama. The audience kills theatre just as the people vilify their state, through indolence, arrogance of power, and spiritual deterioration caused by war. The primary principle of tragic theatre's existence is that a society demands the critical dramatization of its whole self, its larger character. Once this need is no longer supported, theatre is inconceivable.

What kills theatre is not philosophy, which accompanies its creation, but the convincing quality of its performances in a society too weak for the revelations of collective memory. Antonin Artaud has written parallel to this:

We must believe that the essential drama, the one at the root of all the Great Mysteries, is associated with the second phase of Creation, that of the difficulty and of the Double, that of matter and the materialization of that idea.

20. Bruno Snell, *The Discovery of the Mind*, p. 109, points to Aeschylean portrayal of the full freedom to act through decision. This freedom can "turn into a burden, however; with Sophocles already the characters are lonelier than those of Aeschylus." In the Sophoclean context, men act in "deliberate opposition to the world around them. In the end action turns into self-destruction."

It seems indeed that where simplicity and order reign, there can be no theater nor drama, and the true theater, like poetry as well . . . is born out of a kind of organized anarchy after philosophical battles which are the passionate aspect of these primitive unifications.[21]

With the philosophical question of the just ruler, Aeschylus had unfolded his tragic material, and the disappearance of tragic theatre coincided with the growing impossibility of translating his themes (justice and leadership) into "matter." To put it in few words, the theatre persists so long as the city is caught in a tension between its spiritual vision, its need for recollection, and the maintenance of its political order. Once the city moves to eliminate the contradictions between these objectives instead of living with them, its public life shrinks into passivity and empty ceremony. A theatre that is an *audience* can possess no more life than what is revealed in the memory of its spectators. Philosophy does not and cannot end tragedy, it simply continues its questions in different ways, just as Plato in different ways continued the Aeschylean quest for justice in the polis.[22] That Plato censures poetry in his *Republic* is significant for our comparison here, but Havelock has shown how the meaning of poetry for Plato's age was synonymous with a "preserved communication" from Homeric epic, which Plato judged defective as a vehicle for educating citizens to justice and wisdom.[23] Havelock also claims it is dubious that Plato would have equated Aeschylean tragic heroes with the inconsistencies of Homeric ones.

But to say that philosophy carries out the questions of tragedy is not to "explain" the death of tragic theatre. That death, as I am suggesting, is part of the same disintegration that Athens sustains as a city. E. R. Dodds

21. *The Theater and its Double*, tr. M. C. Richards, p. 51.
22. Kenneth Burke, *Grammar of Motives*, p. 230: "Every philosophy is in some respect or other a step away from drama."
23. Eric Havelock, *Preface to Plato*.

best captures this aspect of Greek culture—its potential
for self-destruction:

The disease of which Greek culture eventually died is known by
many names. To some it appears as a virulent form of scepticism;
to others, as a virulent form of mysticism, Professor Murray has
called it the Failure of nerve. My own name for it is systematic
irrationalism. . . . To my mind, the case of Euripides proves that
an acute attack of it was already threatening the Greek world in
the fifth century . . . the peculiar blend of a destructive scepticism
with a no less destructive mysticism; the assertion that emotion,
not reason, determines human conduct; *despair of the state*, resulting in quietism. . . . For the time being, the attack was averted in
part by the development of the Socratic-Platonic philosophy.[24]

Living in a technological age that has abused reason, we can
easily be insensitive to Dodd's explication of Greek "irrationalism." Still, the choice that mattered most for Greek
tragic theatre was not, as for Nietzsche, between the
rational *or* the irrational, but between certain uses of reason
within the new context of the polis. In order to comprehend why Greek theatre perished, then, we have to understand its use of reason and what the theatre, in effect,
communicated while it existed.

The communications of theatre are perhaps the most
threatening to the sacrosanct ego and sense of political
superiority ever to be enshrined in one art form. In
Athens, the major dilemmas of one's life became part of
public speculation and performance. Forgetfulness is the
first refuge of the weary soul, but no theatre audience,
whether it witnessed solemn Aeschylean trilogies or the
brilliant social cartoons of Aristophanes, was allowed this
particular mental shield. The audience was constantly confronted by its own past, unable to elude critical reflection in
action, for the theatre symbolized the continuing interdependence of the two. So long as the art form remained, the
channels to memory would remain open and the city's

---

24. Quoted in Kaufmann, *Tragedy and Philosophy*, p. 300. Emphasis added.

political future would be intricately bound to its former self. This is what is meant by the "theatre as political memory"—a place where the citizen is included in political life not just for his vote or his taxes, but because his memories are part of an on-going polity, part of a public recollection; his city's history, by being "fastened" in his own mind, is actually sustained through his own thoughts and would cease to exist in its unique dimensions if the memory were no longer kept and recalled in public spectacle.

Drama is a unique expression of the polity's highest purpose, and that purpose, like the purpose of man, is not *order* in and for itself but vision and play. When we are sufficiently at ease in the world, we will *act out* our destinies in the form of play rather than pursue the "unlimited" growth of counterfeit material powers. When a political culture has now and then attained a peculiar balance between the requisites of order and the needs of the human psyche, that culture has produced drama in which its inherent violence and tensions are translated into the artist's will to become and the audience's will to remember and act. As the dramatic action becomes a living part of the audience's minds, fulfilling the conscious desire to be entertained, the unconscious desire is to extrapolate something from the performance that will enable us to tolerate the conditions of this world. As Brecht will later suggest, our greatest theatres have always enabled us to satisfy both desires.

Distinguished theatres have been, and are, the cultural wages of discontent—a protest in stage art against the evolutionary, progress-laden themes of ancient political expansions and recent industrial technology. They decry the restless Faustian being in favor of the tragicomic being who accepts the foreclosures of the future in the remembered defeats of the past and in Rilke-fashion transcends by descending into one's own limits, perishing in order to be reborn not as more than mortal but, in accepting mortality, as more than we once were. The theatre, then, enables the audience to experience a kind of political participation that far exceeds that of institutional representation, where the general public retires from the strain of collective responsibility, leaving that burden to a few public servants. The intimidations of memory, as provoked in dramatic art, are, I believe, the main reason for the decline of theatre, for the obligations of recollection and participation on this level become too burdensome. The theatre's powers of education cut through too many defenses; they threaten the one-dimensionality of any polity or community by dramatizing its contemporary reality as merely one alternative in the future of its political life. This renders theatre intolerable for many societies.

Shakespeare will have his Hamlet remark that he would remember his father's ghost as long as "memory has a place in this distracted Globe." When the rare flower of drama at last reappears in that colder island to the north, in the sixteenth century, it will appear first as an alternative political vision, but its preponderant stance will be disenchantment with the purposes and means of political action. Theatre will be obsessed with the dramatization of what will signify a "modern," changing political world: that the solitary individual may accede to political life only *indirectly*.

PART II. The Final Emptiness of Power: Shakespeare and Saint Augustine

Preface to Part II

This study proceeds chronologically through three historical moments of tragic theatre, and it may be instructive here to warn the reader against two deceptively convenient assumptions. The first would be that we are discussing a single tradition of tragic theatre in the history of Europe and America, and that this tradition is characteristic of and idiosyncratic to Western civilization alone. The second assumption would be that tragic theatre becomes more fully developed as an art form the closer we get to the twentieth century, and by implication that theatre before the sixteenth century or outside of Western culture is not as significant.

To the contrary, the purpose of this study has been to both appreciate the singular and unique expressions of politics and dramatic art and to recognize the recrudescence of theatre as a major interpreter of political culture worldwide. So, for example, as Shakespeare begins to write for his Globe Theatre audiences, the theatre of Peking Opera has been in existence for some three centuries. Boisterous and fast-moving, like the Elizabethan stage, Chinese theatre relies on mime, mask, costume, and gesture.[1] Two centuries prior to Elizabethan drama, the magnificent and delicate Noh drama, deriving from Zen Buddhism, is created in fourteenth-century Japan, with action dramatized as in Aeschylean tragedy through memory of longing or regret.[2] Contemporaneous with Shake-

---

1. Leonard Pronko, *Theater East and West*, pp. 44-54.
2. *Ibid.*, pp. 73-108.

spearian drama, Kabuki theatre develops in Japan representing an unusual and beautiful point of contact between
theatres of realism and the more internal and mystical
theatres of the Orient.[3] These instances and others should
alert us to the complex interweavings of public arts that
would seem to be far removed from one another. The
reason we turn to Shakespearian drama in this study,
however, is that the three-century task of nation-building
that would culminate in the predominant political form of
the future, the nation-state, begins in England around the
same period Shakespeare assumes his part in the history of
drama. At the end of Part III we shall return to the present
centrality and significance of Asian theatres in a discussion
of contemporary changes and developments of political
order and drama.

Within theatre's kaleidoscope, the peculiar quality of any
tragic theatre lies in its artistic independence from the host
culture in which it appears. Like Falstaff, it is a heavy
visitor, causing mirth but casting shadows. Unlike Falstaff,
perhaps, it humiliates the host into thinking. It thus tends
to expire in a time proportionate to the popularity of
critical thought: Aeschylus is cut off from his theatre at
the end of his life; Brecht in his youth must flee the host
society; and Shakespeare, though he stands in time between Aeschylus and Brecht, gives us the form of tragic
theatre more familiar to contemporary societies, and cor-
respondingly, the predominantly current vision of political
life.[4] As we shall see, this last statement requires qualification when one considers Shakespeare's answer to the
dilemma of political power, because it is an answer far
more medieval than contemporary.[5] As with Hobbes, we
accept Shakespeare's description of political life, but we

3. *Ibid.*, p. 113.
4. A good exposition of this theme can be found in Jan Kott, *Shakespeare notre
contemporain.* (The English edition is less good.)
5. See E. M. W. Tillyard, *The Elizabethan World Picture.*

impose entirely different solutions, solutions that were known to both Hobbes and Shakespeare and probably abhorred by them.

When considered from the perspective of this study, Shakespeare retains an important likeness to Sophocles, but it is in his notable differences from Aeschylus, from his own unique recreation of political life and its "City of Man," that we learn most about him. Shakespeare created the most contemporary vision of tragic theatre because no dramatist since his time has enlarged upon his vision of the City of Man, although some writers have nobly transmitted its finality and sense of the absurd. By the time Brechtian drama appears in the twentieth century, we are confronted once again with a theatre of political alternatives for altering the fates of nations. This brief preface behind us, our task now is to explore a more despairing dramatic view of the nation.

Shakespeare's England of the late sixteenth century, having taken its Reformation early in 1533 when Luther had just published his first German Bible, had the remainder of the century to tend its wounds—wounds emanating from the dilemma of political authority. J. W. Allen tells us, "The question how such [duly constituted political] authority is derived, on what rests the obligation to obey and how far and in what sense it is limited, was, above all else, the question of the century." As to England's progress in this matter, he writes, "solid success was achieved."[6] Despite this tribute, however, Allen is far more sensitive to the divisions and controversies of the century than he is insistent upon their resolution in any one country of Europe. Indeed, the most obvious aspect of Elizabethan England's "solid success" is that it was the breeding ground for Shakespeare's tragedies. All is not well that ends well if one's cherished traditions have been bartered for success;

6. J. W. Allen, *A History of Political Thought in the 16th Century*, p. 512.

and if ever an artist's memory cleaved to the past inviolably and ineradicably, in the full light of a melancholy present, it was that of Shakespeare. His theatre may be seen as a determined attempt to turn his London and Stratford audiences from all the new science, colonization, and rebellion of the seventeenth century that would unfold, to the painful vision of what would be lost: the "pity, love, and fear" of an old world.

We are familiar with descriptions of the sixteenth and seventeenth centuries: the conflicts between Church and State and between natural theology and new science, represented by Hooker and Bacon as against Galileo, Descartes, and Newton. These centuries reveal the battle of two worlds: one is dying, and the other, far from being too "powerless to be born," is like an overzealous salesman with bag and foot in the door, ready to burst through the old mysterious dwellings. We have to ask why in the midst of this turbulent age the tragic theatre of Shakespeare appears to carry us between sixteenth and seventeenth centuries, somewhat like a voyage across the River Styx; why it assumes its particular form; and to what conditions in the culture and society of England and Europe it owes its spirit and identity.

Frances Yates gives us this accounting: "Elizabethan and Jacobean London was unique in Europe in possessing large numbers of public theatres. Built of wood and able to accommodate thousands of people, these theatres were the wonder of foreign visitors. . . . The prototype of all these new theatres was the one, appropriately called simply 'the Theater,' built by James Burbage in Shoreditch in 1576. . . . And then, as the culmination and crown of all this theatre movement there appeared in Bankside in 1599 the Globe."[7] (We shall discuss the possible reasons for this theatre movement at the end of this Part.)

The Elizabethan bourgeoisie, composing much of the

7. Frances Yates, *Theatre of the World,* pp. 92-93.

Globe's audiences, evolved slowly in the commercial development of England from the thirteenth century, "when
the wool and cloth trade with Flanders and the wine trade
with Bordeaux had started a business expansion which
rapidly swelled in the sixteenth and seventeenth centuries."[8] Shakespeare addressed himself to a mixed public
"more trained in listening than in reading, and more
accustomed to group life than to privacy."[9] Most of Elizabeth's five million subjects were urban, their prosperity
depending upon foreign trade. Their standard of living
was rising, particularly for the yeoman class that produced
among many other literary figures Shakespeare himself.
Alfred Harbage has described the theatre, in this respect,
as "a democratic institution in an intensely undemocratic
age." Class distinctions meant little in the theatre's penny-
a-head cash box. His figures for the towns of Gloucester,
Tewkesbury, and Cirencester in 1608 render the following
social profile of the audiences: gentry, professionals, and
officials, 6.3 percent; dealers and retailers, 19.3 percent;
craftsmen, 52 percent; laborers and carriers, 15 percent;
servants and others, 7.4 percent. Women and students
included, all in all he estimates that 2 out of 15 Londoners
went to the theatre weekly. The audiences were renowned
for their fervent outbursts (one hundred years later, Sir
John Perceval would chide the ladies at a performance of
Othello for being cold, by comparison). In fact, the intensity
of feelings evident in Elizabethan theatre audiences provoked the main criticisms by disquieted public officials.
Theatres were deemed perfect places for "contrivers of
treason and other idele and daungerous persons to meet
together," as if the Elizabethan privileged classes already
sensed that their positions were more secure in precedent
than in their power to preserve them.[10] The theatre here

8. Louis B. Wright, *Middle-Class Culture in Elizabethan England*, p. 5.
9. Boris Ford, ed., *The Age of Shakespeare*, Vol. II, pp. 8-9.
10. A. Harbage, *Shakespeare's Audience*, pp. 14, 52-83, 117-119.

again reveals incipient changes in the polity that can rarely be detected so clearly in other facets of public life.

The drama of England, then, like that of fifth-century Athens, appears in a dynamic, newly urban setting in which political and social structures of the time—in Athens the city, and for England statehood after the Reformation— are in the making and are central to public concern. The actual flow of political, social, and economic life is all-important, consuming, and pervasive. The society wants, at these points, to see where it is going and what it is becoming.[11] In response to that need cities have from time to time reconstituted themselves into theatres. The beginnings of Aeschylean and Shakespearian theatres confirm an apparent optimism that accompanies the early phases of the theatre's creation. Shakespeare's theatre begins energetically to try to resolve the medieval state's break from its transcendent Christian authority by portraying the insufficiency, and eventually the torment, of political power in the absence of absolute love.

Still this optimism is again tempered throughout by an underlying dread of terrible limitations. The tragic undercurrent of sixteenth-century England is foreshadowed in the fifteenth-century cycle plays.

The Biblical drama found no Aeschylus to exalt it into splendor. . . . But though it remained vulgar and crude, we must not underestimate its importance in Shakespeare's background. It was dying out in his day (the last performance of a full cycle was at Coventry in 1580), but it had created a tradition which affected

11. The only period in American history when such a moment might have existed was not at the beginnings of the country's development, but during the Depression of the 1930s, with the Group Theatre in New York, which produced Clifford Odets' *Paradise Lost,* for example. This was a period not filled with national promise and hope, but a time when the nature of national purpose was in question and therefore the first time when the nation as a people could have turned its attention to redeeming a national purpose. But prosperity came too soon, and 50-cent movies made more sense of prosperity than the critical, and more costly, theatre.

both technique and subject matter ... and its use of the most important of all stories had accustomed generations of spectators to assume that drama would have a serious meaning underneath its surface entertainment.[12]

Before we can offer an interpretation of Shakespeare's directions in tragedy in light of his vision of political life, we must attempt to retrace "the serious meaning underneath the surface entertainment." This will take us back to the fourth century A.D. and to the writer who haunts Shakespeare's vision of the external world, St. Augustine.

12. Theodore Spencer, *Shakespeare and the Nature of Man,* p. 53.

5. "The Interim Reading of Life"

The tension or ambivalence that marks the first half of Shakespeare's works is best captured in a phrase by Una Fermor, who calls tragedy "an interim reading of life . . . balancing the 'religious' reading of life against the 'unreligious' reading."[1] Of all the majestic elements in Shakespearian tragedy, perhaps what most distinguishes it is its unparalleled dramatization of this tension between polity and salvation. For the first thing that strikes us as we regard Greek tragedy some twenty centuries later, from the perspective of Shakespeare, is that the entire world of the polis and the political have undergone a monumental transformation severing them from the order of the spirit.

We can locate the more significant departures from the world of classicism in the works of St. Augustine, specifically in terms of three conceptions: knowledge, history, and the state. Charles Cochrane in his *Christianity and Classical Culture* provides an excellent discussion of all three conceptions and gives us this link between the Hellenistic World and the Roman Empire: "Aristotle's successors in the Hellenistic cosmopolis . . addressing themselves to a world of déracinés . . . preached a gospel of purely individual salvation or of salvation in 'society' regarded as *distinct from and independent of political forms.* It was those sects with whose activities the Romans were most familiar . . . and because these threatened 'patriotism,' they were

1. Una Fermor, *The Frontiers of Drama*, quoted in John Danby, *Shakespeare's Doctrine of Nature*, p. 203.

violently repressed."[2] These sects constitute the first real denial of the classical world and its political arrangements. Although Rome was able to suppress them, their ideas soon reappeared in the thought of Augustine to move the masses against the earthly city of their classical heritage.

For Plato, the polis ruled by its best citizens would liberate men from their previous ignorance in a new civic pursuit of wisdom. Knowledge was in this sense not only "a means to 'wisdom' but . . . a source of power" through which men could cultivate their intended natures, for a time at least, in increasing perfection.[3] Augustine, however, did not believe that man could "by reason of any capacity inherent in himself . . . discover a good independent of that which was intrinsic to him as a created being. . . . Thus, for him, the classical ideal of perfectability through knowledge or enlightenment was wholly illusory."[4]

The Thucydidean view of history as recurrent cycles of creation and destruction of cities becomes in the Augustinian framework a single passage to the ultimate disappearance of the earthly city and the everlastingness of God's City. Augustine redefines the Aristotelian purpose of life: instead of "eudamonia," it would be happiness as "beatitude," the intellectual contemplation and love of God. Augustine's view of history demands, as we shall see in the following analysis of his two cities, that the spectacle of history on earth be perceived as tragedy. Prèfaced by original sin, all that is good is fraught with evil, which is merely the lack of an absolute or whole good;[5] and life concludes in total death, except for those who have been granted entrance to the other City. Still, it is a history that

2. Charles Norris Cochrane, *Christianity and Classical Culture,* p. 31. (Emphasis mine.)

3. *Ibid.,* p. 98.

4. *Ibid.,* pp. 451-452.

5. St. Augustine, *City of God,* tr. Walsh *et al.,* XI, 9.

must be played out and will be observed; it is meaningful and purposive even as a voyage of "sickness unto death." In one of his parables, Augustine describes it as "the theatre, the world; the Spectator, God."[6] For Shakespeare, whose sense of the world being a stage was cultivated within the austere atmosphere inherited from Augustine's eschatology, tragic action inevitably occurred in a moral and profoundly spiritual context.

The third conception, that of the state, Augustine preserves within a unique new political theory whose innovation is to place the government of the soul within a far larger constituency than the polis had ever encompassed. After conducting an inquiry into the fall of Rome and all empires or cities before it, Augustine concludes that there is in fact only *one* earthly city no matter when or where it appears. It never constitutes a real "people" in Cicero's sense because it never fulfills its two designated purposes: justice and peace. Thus it always perishes from pollution and civil war. Augustine's most significant condemnation of the classical world's political forms (all of which he refers to as the one *civitas terrena, civitas diaboli,* or City of Man) is that they are fragile: they all too quickly pass from foundation to disintegration.[7] The political state is unendurable merely as an example of order, but it has unqualifiedly no regenerative powers over man's nature. Far from self-sufficient, it is founded in fratricide, in perpetual decay, and dependent for its very authority upon the higher order of which it forms a part. This Augustinian view of the political state is paralleled by Shakespeare's outlook as he canvassed English history in his Chronicle plays, at a time when Europe was commencing its three-century task of nation-building. The question that cuts through these plays, from first to last, is: what in this world can bind the

6. *The Political Writings of St. Augustine,* ed. H. Paolucci, p. 159.
7. *City of God,* I, XV, XVIII.

state together and still be worthy of loyalty? Shakespeare, like Augustine, is preoccupied with the human implications of order on the earth—an order which is not simply external to the human soul but which reflects its essential needs and conflicts. And Shakespeare seems to fear at the outset, as Augustine had known, that the earthly city thrives on the "imperial theme," or power pursued for its own sake. Earthly order seems to endure in constant injustice, like a body that would appear to flourish in its own decay.

However, the former Greek preoccupation with securing a proper and specific constitution within the polis was, for Augustine, clearly secondary. Since the destiny of the civitas terrena was death and extinction, political forms retained a limited significance; they were to preserve communication between man and the City of God. If the political authority transgressed God's commandments, each man had the choice of refusing to act, of not cooperating, for the political state did not deserve man's highest loyalty even though the well-ordered state was definitely a great virtue.[8] The voluntary self-denial of action was in fact the only real human power in the City of Man. (This will be of consequence when later we discuss Hamlet and Lear.) The entire dimension of action in the City of Man is deeply suspect. Prompted by the desire for praise, it ineluctably serves unscrupulous self-interest.[9] Augustine put it most poignantly in one phrase that we might have suspected to issue from Hamlet's own murmurings: "the answer is, that what is here required is not a bodily action, but an inward disposition."[10] In Shakespeare's day, subject as it was to the frankness of Machiavelli's thought, the very notion of political action, connoted by the word "policy," stood for what the "Germans dignified by the name Realpolitik, that is

8. The Political Writings of St. Augustine, p. 351.
9. City of God, XIV, 28.
10. Saint Augustine, Contra Faustum, XXII, 74-79.

political action which ignores all moral considerations."[11]

Bearing in mind Augustine's departure from classical political thought, as sketched in the preceding pages, it is only when we consider the uniqueness of his theory of two cities in light of its psychology of love that we move into the center of Shakespeare's conception of the political and of tragedy itself. The two cities are two fundamentally opposed associations, which "have been formed, therefore, by two loves: the earthly by love of self, even to contempt of God; the heavenly by love of God, even to contempt of self."[12] Love of God and love of self are entirely discrete and contrary. The man who lives by the first is part of the City of God. The man who lives by the second is forever exiled from the Heavenly City. Most important from Augustine's perspective, the terror of being isolated from God's City is not as great after death as it is while we endure this life; and there is not a single tragedy by Shakespeare that does not dwell upon this terror of the excluded absolute. The only sense of measure the City of Man possesses is nowhere within itself but is a temporary gift from the City of God. Thus the City of Man apart from the heavenly City is adrift in a void, imperiled, drunk with unreality, and unequipped to judge the difference between appearance and essence. This isolated City of Man is the source of all human injustice and tragedy, simply the existence of mistaken love. "This injustice is seen in every case where a man loves for their own sake things which are desirable only as means to an end, and seeks for the sake of something else things which ought to be loved for themselves. For thus, as far as he can, he disturbs in himself the natural order which the eternal law requires us to observe."[13]

The pain Lear suffers is very nearly contained in these

11. Edwin Muir, *The Politics of King Lear*, p. 16.
12. *City of God*, XIV, 28.
13. *Ibid.*

lines. Augustine is claiming that we can disturb the natural
order of all life in the universe simply through the wrong
sort of love, and the reason lies in this: between love of God
and love of self is the difference between a love that binds
the community together and a love that turns it into a war
of all against all. Thus, if the amor-sui of civitas terrena,
emanating from greed and individual interest alone, is the
only love that fills the City of Man, that city will know no
respite from permanent chaos and disunity.

For Augustine, the entire significance of the human city,
however, is that it becomes in his framework the arena for
these contesting loves. The City of Man does serve a divine
purpose if it provides the environment in which man can
perceive his soul's dependence upon amor-Dei. The well
ordered City of Man can provide an astonishing but ideal
combination of rule: that of political power and absolute
love. In this sense, Augustine is far more absorbed in the
necessity of governance and rule in the City of Man that he
is in rendering the reality of God's City. He has already
shown us the self-destructive effects of political power in
the history of the state. But his point transcends the fact of
power's corruption on the earth and rises to the fact that
power of itself has no sustenance. Earthly power is, in
effect, as powerless as mortality is against immortality. The
very trappings of terrestrial kingdom and realm are at best
the imperfect reflection of God's order in his City based
upon his all-consuming love for man. Political power in the
absence of God's love is illusory and paltry; it is nothing.

Out of this pessimism, Augustine permits the earthly city
a limited but extraordinary significance. It will be the play
within the play; as in the case of Shakespeare's finest exploration of this theme, in *Hamlet,* the inner play does not
remove the evil, but it does reveal it, providing a sense of
measure that is far from purposeless. Although the conception of God's City had already been dissolving in the
European consciousness of Shakespeare's time, one can

furnish the two greatest themes of Shakespeare's theatre from the following passage in Augustine's *City of God*: "I have already said, in previous Books, that God had two purposes in deriving all men from one man. His first purpose was to give unity to the human race by likeness of nature. His second purpose was to bind mankind by the bond of peace, through blood relationship, into one harmonious whole."[14] Shakespeare's tragedies do confirm both a common humanity on the earth and the need to create from this a spiritual unity amongst men, but with one overwhelming difference—these themes would no longer float between Augustine's two cities. They would have to be confined now to the isolated City of Man, to the city of power without the city of binding love, and for this Shakespeare would have to introduce his own political vision.

Although Arthur dies in Shakespeare's *King John* and with him dies the "truth" of the old world, it is hoped that a reconciliation of keen tactics and innocent love in the figure of Henry V may yet be believable. It is in this Machiavellian posture—of rediscovering political value in the isolated City of Man—that Shakespeare embarks upon his history plays. We will begin with a rendering of some of these plays in an attempt to reconstruct Shakespeare's aspirations for the ideal secular ruler and his eventual disillusionment with any but a formal, Renaissance political solution for the sorrows of this fragmented world. As T. S. Eliot has urged, we will try to be sensitive to Shakespeare's works as a whole but will approach the various spheres in his development remembering that, unlike Aeschylus' single and unified progression, Shakespeare begins with far less hope, turns from even that, and then at the last prefers to celebrate the very loss of that other world than to abandon this one forever to silence and modernity.

14. *Ibid.*, XIV, 1.

6. Power Without Love

Political power in Shakespeare's history or chronicle plays (*Henry VI, Richard III, King John, Richard II, Henry IV,* and *Henry V*)[1] is best understood as conceived in Machiavelli's *Prince* and *Discourses*: a manifestation of secular territory and rule that permits the realization of two political ideals— national unity and the pageantry of heroic action. This is a conception of power as much dramatic as political; the way in which its effects are staged and the Prince's awareness that he is the leading actor in a continuing drama of his state can be decisive for his retention of political power. Renaissance populaces, accustomed to centuries of symbolic and allegorical interpretation of civic and religious life, would be quick to perceive polities, whenever appropriate, as theatres. As we shall see later, when the discussion turns to an emergence of Renaissance theatre itself from medieval street tableaux and processionals, the relationship between monarchical display of power and dramatic shows is firmly established.

Machiavelli's insight does not lie so much in his vivid portrayal of strategies for seizing royal power as in his comprehension of power's frailty once achieved. He knew, as did Augustine, that purely secular power is a dependent and not an independent phenomenon; therefore, once the Prince has made his conquest, the holding of that power becomes a very different matter indeed. Often the maintenance of power will require concessions to the people,

1. Listed in the chronological order of their composition.

mercy and liberality. In any event, legitimization of power once established will constitute *the* problem for the ruler, and it is the dramatic task for Shakespeare as he writes his first history play, *Henry VI.* In a reading of the history plays in sequence, one first observes that the problem confronting us at the outset remains unresolved throughout: royal power is defective and illegitimate, and its exercise is utilitarian at best and always culminates in divisions: "The situation under Henry IV was similar to that under the Tudors, for the same uncertainty of the right of the king to reign, the same conflict over the succession, the same threat of foreign interference, and the same need for a strong central authority existed at the beginning of the Wars of the Roses as at their close."[2]

Shakespeare's portrayal of kingship does not fill us with confidence, perhaps any more than did the latter part of Elizabeth's reign. Though England suffered no invasion during her rule, it did fight in Scotland, Ireland, in France for Henry IV, and in the Netherlands against Spain. Elizabeth was especially fearful of war with Spain in 1598, and for that time spent an enormous amount entirely on defense.[3] Shakespeare's preoccupation with civil war and rebellion, especially in *Henry IV,* is very much a response to actual Elizabethan policy; and his obsession with the "killing of the king"[4] is more than reflection on the past when one considers that 43 years after Shakespeare's most despairing composition, *King Lear,* the English people would decapitate Charles I.

As we enter the world of *Henry VI,* we discover the "regulating principle of traditional society . . . mercy, pity, love, human kindness, reinforced by God's ordinating fiat" still intact.[5] Yet Henry VI, as ruler, embodies the fundamental

2. Lily B. Campbell, *Shakespeare's Histories. Mirror of Elizabethan Policy,* pp. 215-216.

3. *Ibid.,* p. 257.

4. John F. Danby, *Shakespeare's Doctrine of Nature,* p. 60.

5. *Ibid.*

heresy of Machiavelli's political world: he cannot tell appearance from reality and moreover does not see the necessity for such a discriminating perception. For this reason his traditional society in the newly isolated City of Man is no match for the diabolical stratagems of Richard III. "Thus we are confronted with a king who takes satisfaction in making the gestures of royalty but who remains unaware of the substructure of political mastery which must underlie the grand act, if it is to achieve anything of permanent value."[6] There has rarely been a more overwhelming vision of tragedy than the one in which Shakespeare shows us the traditional king who unwittingly enacts the perished maxims of an age long past within the framework of a new, efficient, clever, and vicious age of which he has no inkling whatsoever. In this light, all of Shakespeare's histories are but a prelude to *Lear*. And they all anticipate the final despair that there is little political redemption within the conflict of two worlds: one dying, and the other too absorbed with power to admit the healing force of unselfish love.

In *Richard III*, Shakespeare gives us for the first time the epitome of the political divorced from the spiritual and power divorced from love in the City of Man.[7] Even at the close of *Henry VI, Part III*, Richard then Duke of Gloucester exclaims: "And this word 'love', which greybeards call divine, Be resident in men like one another, And not in me: I am myself alone" (V. vi. 70). For Richard III, there is only one theme to life, that which Macbeth will call "the Imperial theme"—to wear the Crown by any means. For the first time, English audiences would be confronted with the regicide of a good king for all his faults, and the

6. H. M. Richmond, *Shakespeare's Political Plays*, p. 34.

7. Thomas Jameson refers to "the central dilemma of Rule—power divorced from love," in *The Hidden Shakespeare; A Study of the Poet's Undercover Activity in the Theater*, pp. 95-96.

success of a villian who, instead of suffering immediate and appropriate punishment for his deed, will wear the Crown. Although he ultimately meets with violent death, nothing can erase the profound dilemma of Richard's success. As with Edmund in *Lear,* "there is the recognition that the principle symbolized by Henry VI is clearly a false-consciousness."[8]

One inescapable conclusion of *Richard III* is that in a world without the binding force of absolute love, the *cupiditas* or selfish love of Man's City only assists the determined evil. Love of self, or romantic love as Shakespeare often portrays it, only blurs the senses permitting the evil to operate through jealousy and poor vision, as in *Troilus and Cressida* and *Othello.* Erotic love is crippling because one still believes desire is based upon an ideal; this is the sorrow of Lady Anne's involvement with Richard. At first, when she protests Richard's murder of Henry VI, who was "gentle, mild, and virtuous!", he responds, "The fitter for the King of Heaven, that hath him" (I. ii. 105). She cannot reconcile Richard's passion with his contempt; for while he wants to possess the world *so much,* she realizes at the same time that he believes nothing is above debasement within it, including herself. The fact that only the evil enjoy possession of the City of Man is what is so disconcerting in *Richard III.* The sweeter natures, like Hamlet and Cordelia, in the face of unthinkable deeds, will sicken of the world, fail to act, and do not relish worldly possession.

The dilemma clearly emerging from *Richard III* is that the Machiavellian virtues, of judgment beyond appearance and commitment to political action, have become the efficient arsenal of a determined villain rather than the qualities of a noble and heroic kingship. Shakespeare will attempt in the successive histories to achieve a blend

8. John F. Danby, *Shakespeare's Doctrine of Nature,* p. 73.

somewhere between the ruthless use of power and its purely benevolent use in order to preserve Machiavelli's framework of perception and heroic action, but the blend will come at too high a price—the mediocrity and vapidity of Henry V.

In *King John* and *Richard II*, Shakespeare continues to place before us the issue of legitimizing the illegitimate succession. *King John* and later *Henry V* represent definite turning points in his examination of political power. With the first play, he exhausts the slightest faith in reestablishing a medieval regalism; with the latter, he abandons any constructive alternative for the political world of force and interest. Between these two plays, he is seeking a man to fulfill the requisites of secular kingship, but he sees the world too much as it has become to deliver happy endings where they are no longer welcome. In *King John,* we witness a final erosion of that other city of absolute love and compassion. It is expressed, as in *Lear,* by the articulate bastard who reveals the inner thread of the play:

> Commodity, the bias of the world; . . .
> The bawd, this broker, this all-changing word,
> Clapt on the outward eye of fickle France,
> Hath drawn him from his own determined aid,
> From a resolved and honourable war,
> To a most base and vile-concluded peace . . .
> Since kings break faith upon commodity,
> Gain, be my lord, - for I will worship thee!
>   (II. i. 574-98)

Here in one brief step, the world of "gain" substitutes itself in full for all that once had commanded human loyalty: God, love, king, community.[9] The strongest forces at work in *Lear* have already been acknowledged by the Bastard Faulconbridge. After Arthur's death, he gives us this astonishing message:

---

9. It is informative, in terms of this, to read Weber's analysis of the diminishing impact of "brotherliness" as it clashes with a money-centered, rational world in Gerth and Mills, *From Max Weber,* pp. 331-340.

From forth this morsel of dead royalty,
The life, the right, and truth of all this realm
Is fled to heaven; and England now is left
To tug and scamble, and to part by th' teeth
The unowed interest of proud-swelling state.
(IV. iii. 143-47)

With more than a little disenchantment, the remaining history plays (*Richard II*, *Henry IV*, and *Henry V*) constitute Shakespeare's attempt to provide political alternatives for the order that passes with Arthur's life.

In a sense, Shakespeare's tragic theatre is permanently traumatized by the magnetic cruelty of Richard III, who is in effect Shakespeare's Callicles. Shakespeare never met to his own satisfaction the challenge of Richard's derision. He never produced a "good" king that quite equalled the intelligence, the fascination, or the worldly self-confidence of Richard III. And the sorrow of *Richard II*, where Shakespeare does explore for the last time the possibilities of a completely virtuous and intelligent king, is that the rules of secular kingship no longer seem to allow these distinctions any relevance. There are no good kings or bad kings; there is only the system that affords no freedom from the "wheel of fire."[10] As Jan Kott suggests, in Shakespeare's world political power exists in a vacuum apart from compassion, and the world is always stronger than men, whose values are consumed in its presence and indifference.[11] In the City of Man, all men are equally subject to the human condition, but a beggar is more fortunate than the king who still believes he can rule that city without becoming crushed by it. Shakespeare conveys this ultimate skepticism in Richard II's famous soliloquy on the subject:

For within the hollow crown
That rounds the mortal temples of a king
Keeps Death his cout; and there the antick sits,
Scoffing his state, and grinning at his pomp . . .

10. Jan Kott, *Shakespeare notre contemporain*, p. 25.
11. *Ibid.*, p. 63.

As if this flesh, which walls about our life
Were brass impregnable; and humour'd thus
Comes at the last, and with a little pin
Bores through his castle-wall . . .
. . . throw away respect,
Tradition, form, and ceremonious duty;
For you have but mistook me all this while:
I live with bread like you, feel want,
Taste grief, need friends: - subjected thus,
How can you say to me, I am a king?

(III. ii. 161-78)

We have in this passage the sixteenth-century dilemma of ruler and state: what will constitute legitimate authority in the solitary City of Man? With the abdication of its medieval religious grounding, what will distinguish the King from any man who can seize the Crown? Shakespeare's portrayal of royal authority is paraphrased by Burckhardt's description of the Italian states of the fifteenth century: "The foundation of the system was and remained illegitimate, and nothing could remove the curse which rested upon it."[12]

It is clear that if something might have served as ground for legitimate political authority, it was not to be found in Richard II's aloof and scholarly style. Although his character and intent are noble, virtue is not sufficient for the "speciality of rule,"[13] as we learn from the good Brutus in *Julius Caesar,* who is persuaded to justify treason and the murder of a friend. Ruling is an art that demands objective and constant vigilance over the needs of state. Richard II is too absorbed in thought to render full devotion to political action (a familiar Shakespearian distraction). Richard is overthrown not because he abuses authority, but because he makes less popular use of it than his usurper. Holinshed explains that Henry Bolingbroke could not have usurped Richard II's throne without the ready support of the people; only this would make possible "the deposing of

12. Jacob Burckhardt, *The Civilization of the Renaissance in Italy,* p. 10.
13. Ulysses' words in *Troilus and Cressida.*

their rightful and naturall prince king Richard, whose cheefe fault rested onlie in that . . . he was too bountifull to his friends, and too mercifull to his foes."[14]

Richard II is as much a Christian king as Shakespeare ever created (despite Henry V's allusion to himself as such), and Shakespeare's suggestion as to that king's fate is prophetic from the point of view of England's seventeenth century. The success of Henry IV and the subsequent national unification under Henry V confirm that the strongest basis for legitimate authority in the future City of Man would lie in the ruler's capacities for persuasion. Shakespeare could hardly have greeted this insight with optimism, predisposed as he was to reserve the speciality of rule to two alternatives alone: either rightful kingship or no rule whatsoever. In the latter case, as with Henry IV and Henry V, the state was appropriated at the levels of instrumentality and salesmanship. These aspects of Henry IV's new state are evident in the last scenes of *Richard II*. When Bolingbroke (Henry IV) condemns Richard to exile and forced separation from his wife, she implores: "Banish us both, and send the king with me." The Earl of Northumberland responds, "That were some love, but little policy" (V. i. 84).

Henry IV is a man so profoundly cold by nature that only through the frequent intervention of allegory and imagery of the sun is Shakespeare's audience able to withstand the chill.[15] Falstaff's tavern is such welcome relief from the dreary Court. "The world we see is one that has disintegrated into mutually exclusive spheres—the worlds of Court, of the tavern, of Shallow's Gloucestershire, of the rebellious lords."[16] The same *civitas terrena* that had secured independence from the City of God suffers now further secessions; the center does not hold. Henry IV is

---

14. Quoted in Thomas Jameson, *The Hidden Shakespeare*, p. 56.
15. Jameson, in *Hidden Shakespeare*, pp. 95-96, refers to the sun imagery in *Henry IV*.
16. John F. Danby, *Shakespeare's Doctrine of Nature*, p. 83.

an appropriate man to govern such pools of privacy and interest. In his pathetic relationship with his son, we get a glimpse of his ability for political calculation and tactics. The more unloving, remote, and perfunctory he is as a father, the more he appears well-suited to the main quality of secular politics: rational opportunism.

As Henry IV dies, he evaluates his own rule in these words to the young prince: "God knows, my son, By what by-paths and indirect crookt ways I met this crown; and I myself know well How troublesome it sat upon my head: To thee it shall descend with better quiet, Better opinion, better confirmation" (*Part II,* IV, iv, 314-19). These last words seem more fitting for an exchange of Boards of Directors than for the supreme transfer of political authority of the state, from father to son. As John Danby suggests, Hal's last scene with his father implies that the succession is nothing but the transfer of mere property in the "realm."[17] Until his last breath, Henry IV preserves his concern for the appearances of royal power. His supposition that his son will enjoy "better confirmation" is based upon his insight into the modern political populace. It will grant Henry V more of a consensus simply because he is more removed from the initial iniquitous act. Henry IV's state, like the many European and American electorates, is governed by formation of mass opinion and public images which often have nothing to do with political realities. In order to insure his good image against past transgressions, Henry IV's final recommendation to his son is to "foment foreign quarrels" to turn the people's attention from their own domestic situation. This all-too-familiar contemporary strategy for diverting political criticism casts a rather dubious light upon the forthcoming capacities of Henry V for responsible and exemplary kingship. Moreover, it does not occur to the dying Henry IV that if rule by popular

17. *Ibid.*, p. 88.

support may at one point in history assure the succession of a usurper-king, it may at another point just as easily eliminate kingship altogether. But Shakespeare spares him, in his final hours, such nightmares of democracy.

If Henry V is Shakespeare's portrayal of his ideal king, as some critics have argued, one may well be baffled by the unpromising faults he places in the youthful Henry. To begin with, there is his somewhat callous dispensing with an old friend, Falstaff, at the end of *Henry IV, Part II:*

> I know thee not, old man: fall to thy prayers . . .
> I have long dreamed of such a kind of man,
> So surfeit-swell'd, so old, and so profane;
> But, being awaked, I do despise my dream . . .
> For God doth know, so shall the world perceive,
> That I have turn'd away my former self;
>
> (V. v. 49-59)

Here is a most curious assumption of royal power and personal maturation. Henry V, whose escapades have earned him no distinction whatever, will prove his royal bearing by denying his former self, its friendships and secrets. As one reexperiences this play, the spectacle of Henry's newly sculpted and plastic expression as he addresses Falstaff troubles the reader. With self-righteous arrogance, he declares to his former friend: "Till then, I banish thee, on pain of death." And all this, remembering that aside from what may be a legitimate rejection of values and behavior, the friendship tendered Hal by Falstaff was the only friendship the new king had ever known. How easily it was bartered for a mere gesturing of power.

There is more than a hint of irony in the opening lines between the Bishop of Ely and the Archbishop of Canterbury describing the new king:

> Never was such a sudden scholar made;
> Never came reformation in a flood,
> With such a heady current, scouring faults;
>
> (I. i. 32-34)

Henry V is the new rationalist, the self-made king, with no illusions about the world of appearance that had so baffled Henry VI. Early in the play, conspirators boldly affront the king with their hypocrisy:

> . . . there's not, I think, a subject
> That sits in heart-grief and uneasiness
> Under the sweet shade of your government.
>
> (II. ii. 24-25)

But Henry is quick to find them out, and faster still to sentence them to death. Henry V is a man of action. He has the imposing manner and willfullness of a Henry VIII. He has the appeal of a dynamic executive, the Tudor appeal of sheer stability—he knows how to hold on to what he wants, for himself and for England.

The first sense Shakespeare gives us of Henry V's political objectives comes in Act I: Henry claims: "We are no tyrant, but a Christian king" (ii. 242). This statement concludes a dreary prospectus for recovering land from France, whose original ownership is dubious at best, in an attempt to unify England against potential civil war (doubtless the first effort to implement his father's earlier suggestion). The scenario is filled with homilies of strategy like this one spoken by the Earl of Westmoreland:

> If that you will France win,
> Then with Scotland first begin:
>
> (I. ii. 168)

Henry's political outlook is expansive. He will secure stable order and prosperity in his realm by subduing France. If we keep in mind that this play precedes the founding of the first English colony in America (1604) by just a few years, we can more readily anticipate the political form that takes shape in *Henry V*, one that will serve as model for the rest of the world—the imperialistic nation-state. Of this, there is much more to say, but it is enlightening for Shakespeare's representation of political power in relation to the state to recall here one of Weber's reflections on that subject:

All political structures use force, but they differ in the manner in which and the extent to which they use or threaten to use it against other political organizations. These differences play a specific role in determining the form and destiny of political communities. Not all political structures are equally "expansive." They do not all strive for an outward expansion of their power, or keep their force in readiness for acquiring political power over other territories and communities by incorporating them or making them dependent. Hence, as structures of power, political organizations vary in the extent to which they are turned outward.[18]

The precedent established in *Henry V* is that of the emerging nation-state defined in terms of its expansive uses of political power. The English nation will achieve unification by external conquest—a precedent of ancient empires that appears slow to die; and with this outward expansion of power comes a more lonely kingship. Henry V's self-portrait is one of the misunderstood and anxious monarch who alone, against the world, must secure the domain:

> The slave, a member of the country's peace,
> Enjoys it; but in gross brain little wots
> What watch the king keeps to maintain the peace,
> Whose hours the peasant best advantages.
>   (IV. i. 285-288)

How far the world of Henry V is removed from the two cities of Augustine, from the comforting medieval divine construction, from the Christian Kings as happy in tempering "with mercy and generosity the inevitable harshness of their decrees,"[19] from the single human community as the reflection of God's harmonious universe.

The subterranean current of irony prevails throughout

18. Gerth and Mills, *From Max Weber,* p. 159.
19. *City of God,* V, 24.

Henry V, to the very end. In Hollywood fashion, the gallant and victorious king wins his desired queen, but the concluding chorus informs us that their son will be crowned as a child, that he will lose France, and will make England bleed. We are left to ponder, as always with Shakespeare, the fate of kings, but this time we are more pointedly invited to consider the destiny of this new and apparently successful political form of the nation-state.[20] It should be noted that Shakespeare employs the prologue and epilogue choruses solely in *Henry IV* and *Henry V.* We know, from the origins of the chorus in Greek tragedy that the choral function is developed essentially in relation to the needs of political education, that it draws the dialogue of the play to those elements touching the community as a whole, and that it counteracts the specific bias of specific actors. The chorus is the actor whose orientation is always total. Shakespeare's use of the chorus, then, is indicative of his intention to have these plays teach us something about the political character of Henry V's polity and perhaps warn us as well of its irrevocable lack of authenticity.

With this final history play, Shakespeare has completed his journey from the City of Man's genesis in God's love and preeminence to its modern foundation upon pure domination. From a delicate balance of absolute sovereignty, common law, and control of rebellious religious factions, the new English state, on a keynote of economic individualism, was to become the world's "first modernizer."[21] Shakespeare's theatre is intimately shaped by his vision of this modern state and particularly by his evalua-

---

20. Samuel Huntington quotes (from McIlwain's *High Court*): "The England of the Tudors was an 'organic state' to a degree unknown before Tudor times, and forgotten almost immediately afterward." Then he comments: "After the brief interlude of the Marian struggles, however, the shrewd politicking and popular appeal of Elizabeth restored a peace among religious groups which was virtually unique in Europe at that time." (*Political Order in Changing Societies,* pp. 124-125.)

21. Huntington, *Political Order,* p. 46.

tion of its future. One will recall that Shakespeare approaches all that is political from an essential pessimism; throughout his history plays, he is experimenting with the nature of secular power divorced from its ground of legitimacy in absolute love, and his disposition toward secular political authority is one of suspicion and disillusionment. He perceives political power as a moral problem from the beginning, and the sole resolution he offers us in *Henry V* is that the Hobbesian world of power and appetite must be ruled by a strong sovereign of charismatic appeal. This conclusion is a product of the general demoralization of his society and a confession on Shakespeare's part, as a dramatist, that tragic art can do nothing to divert the principle of decay inherent in secular politics. But he can record it with unmerciful accuracy; he can show the spiritual regression that will accompany the brave new homo-economicus and his imperial state; he can create *King Lear*.

The answers to the questions of legitimacy and spiritual loss raised in the history plays are all to be found in *Lear*, and we will proceed to look for them in that play in order to appreciate Shakespeare's final estimation of the modern political state, and in which direction his tragic theatre is thereby impelled. For Robert Speaight, *Henry V* constitutes a "watershed" in Shakespeare's work. Up to that point, Shakespeare had been concentrating on the use and abuses of authority; afterwards he shows us its "abdication."[22] It is from this perspective that we approach *King Lear*, as the human tragedy which issues from an abdication of political authority.

Before we move on to *Lear*, however, it may be well to get our chronological bearings. The last two history plays had been composed between 1597 and 1600. In 1597, Shakespeare buried his only son, Hamnet, at the age of seven

22. Robert Speaight, "Shakespeare and Politics," p. 16.

years.[23] Various Shakespeare biographies (like the passionate work of Rouse) would indicate that Shakespeare was permanently shaken by his son's death. Without the hope of a surviving son, a tragedian who lamented the barter of a traditional world for that of commodity, as Shakespeare did, was likely to feel even more alien in the newly atomized universe of the seventeenth century. From the evidence of Shakespeare's own will and various lawsuits during his lifetime,[24] it would appear that he was extremely protective of his daughters and grandchild, and that his conduct with his children was tender and responsible. These things may be significant for our understanding of the starkness his tragedies convey after 1600 and his tendency to focus upon the desperate relationships between parents and children.

In 1600, the conspirators against Elizabeth—Essex and Shakespeare's own patron, Southhampton—were hanged. Whether Shakespeare fully sympathized with their rebellion or not, the state's execution of his friend and patron must have lent bitter substance to the line that would characterize his most famous tragedy, composed in the following year. Was it an accident that he altered the setting of *Hamlet,* or was there something rotting in the state of England, and was its dramatist at pains to disguise his report? *Hamlet* is the first of several tragedies after the turn of the century vastly more despairing than Shakespeare's previous work. A door seems to close on the past and even more tightly on the future, and one is "left with nothing to call one's own but death."[25]

King Lear was performed in 1606 for the first time,[26] when Hobbes as a young boy may have been amongst the astonished spectators, and when the Elizabethan age had finally expired. Whether Hobbes ever viewed a scene of

---

23. F. E. Halliday, *The Life of Shakespeare,* pp. 130-31.
24. *Ibid.,* pp. 130-150 *passim.*
25. From *Richard II* (III, ii, 153).
26. Edwin Muir, *The Politics of King Lear,* p. 7.

Lear, he did eventually capture the essence of its kingdom of darkness in his own political theory some fifty years afterwards. Shakespeare sketches in *Lear* the Hobbesian principle of history and politics which Hobbes will derive from its first author, Thucydides. This is a principle shared also by Burckhardt, who "believed that in human affairs reason plays only a small part, while man's struggle for power greatly affects the course of events."[27] Within the framework of *Lear*, we witness the conflict of two conceptions of society, where the "pity, love, and fear" of a medieval universe are devoured by contests for power in a continuous and "shallow" present.

What is most significant about *Lear*'s internal polarity is not the outcome of the conflict, which despite its brutality would have come as no surprise to the seventeenth-century Globe's audience of one or two thousand persons. Rather, it is the very resistance to that outcome which Shakespeare so willingly portrays in recalling the clearly abandoned medieval world of Lear and Cordelia. Here, as in his last plays, Shakespeare is capable of imposing that ancient hope of love in its absolute Augustinian version, upon of all places the brave new world of Edmund, whose society has no tolerance for anything aging let alone medieval, and no memory beyond the immediate and mechanistic satisfaction of impulsive desires. We have to realize that Lear was an antique, however fond and foolish, at the time Shakespeare created him. Similarly, we must imagine this antique as existing not within the medieval hierarchy of his rational delirium in the first Act, but as he is thrust permanently out of time into Edmund's society, which drives him through madness to a denial of reason's very existence. Edmund is the embodiment of "the new age of scientific inquiry, industrial development, bureaucratic organization and social regimentation . . . of monopoly

27. Reinhard Bendix, *Max Weber and Jacob Burckhardt*, p. 176.

and Empire-making . . . an age of competition, suspicion and glory."[28] The point is that Shakespeare wants us to see this all-too-apparent new world through Augustine's stained-glass, through the relic of pomp and ceremony, and through the medieval king's abdication of authority in an impossible exchange for eternal love. Our question is this: why, in one of his last and greatest tragedies, does he reconstruct the ancient loss, the pain, and the love?

One of the answers comes in the play's puzzling and convulsive first Act. It is a hint that Augustine's two cities were not so much lost as forsaken by the old monarchies. Both Gloucester and Lear, the older generation, appear conspicuously irresponsible in this Act.[29] Irresponsibility epitomizes the pathetic jests Gloucester puts forth to account for the existence of his bastard son, Edmund. But with Lear, irresponsibility is much more total; the entire play is devoted to its ensuing chaos. The nature of that irresponsibility is evident in his first lines:

> . . . Know that we have divided
> In three our kingdom; and 'tis our fast intent
> To shake all cares and business from our age,
> Conferring them on younger strengths while we
> Unburdened crawl towards death.
>
> (I. i. 37–41)

Lear, in these words, is divesting himself of rule, which he loosely defines as "interest of territory, cares of state" (I. i. 50), in order to "unburden" himself in his old age—to be cared for, as he trusts, by his children and the state. It is a form of retirement, and it has the same sort of logic as Lear's intention to divide the kingdom so "that future strife May be prevented now" (I. i. 43–44). Lear is interested in avoiding future conflict and obligations, and he has struck

28. John F. Danby, *Shakespeare's Doctrine of Nature*, p. 46.
29. The interpretation of *Lear* offered here owes much to Stanley Cavell's fine piece on Lear, entitled "The Avoidance of Love," in *Must We Mean What We Say? A Book of Essays*.

upon a ready solution of conferring the "cares" and "business" upon "younger strengths," dividing the kingdom's territory amongst his three daughters according to the extent in verbal expression of each girl's love for her father. But Lear's actions, which have all the modern logic of retirement and inheritance, are staged within the medieval political world of Augustine's two cities; on that stage, these actions have no logic but that of authority's abdication.

We have only to remember the significance of a unified kingdom for Shakespeare's history plays to understand the sort of deviation that is involved in Lear's desire, as king, to divide his kingdom as rewards for his children's love.[30] This is not Augustine's portrait of rulership, which emphasized a ruler's commitment to the City of God and to its selfless protection in the City of Man, not the disinterested rule that demanded a unique combination of political power and God's love. The king derived his authority from his obligation to preserve that combination. Nothing in the City of Man, of itself, had priority over the salvation of each soul in God's transcendent community. It is in this setting that Lear's actions reveal an irresponsibility that had probably been present throughout his life as husband, father, and king. For Lear is thinking too little of his political subjects, for whom a divided kingdom will mean injustice and chaos (which in principle it often will in Shakespeare's tragedies). And he is not thinking too clearly of his children, because he renders the highest gifts to the least deserving and rewards the only love with anger and banishment.

30. An argument can certainly be made that Lear believed he was resolving the inevitable property squabble in the only way possible, before his death, given the absence of a male heir to the kingdom. But he does not seem to have weighed sufficiently, in his mind, the enormous burden this would place upon the youngest daughter who would inherit the "choicest morcel," any more than he realized the burden he was placing upon her by his simple question in this scene. Therefore, at the outset, the tragedy unfolds as simultaneously political and personal, a characteristically Shakespearian beginning.

Painfully, one admits that Lear is a selfish man, and it is his self-love that lies at the root of his tragedy: misjudgment. From Goneril, we hear that "the best and soundest of his time hath been but rash" (i. i. 294-295). But it is, as usual, from the Fool that we discover the full dimension of Lear's misjudgment:

> ... e'er since thou mad'st thy
> daughters thy mothers; for when tho gav'st them the
> rod, and put'st down thine own breeches,
> Then they for sudden joy did weep,
> And I for sorrow sung,
> That such a king should play bo-peep
> And go the fools among.
>
> (I. iv. 163-169)

One will recall Augustine's insight that the wrong sort of love can de-nature any part of the City of Man. In making his children a parent over himself and in his desire to eschew the weighty cares and reversals of rule, Lear wants "the appurtenance without the responsibility of kingship."[31]

We have the feeling now of having been through this before, and of course we have, with *Henry VI*. But Henry VI's penchant for estimating too highly the world of appearance lacks the particular innovation Lear adopts as he proposes the remarkable exchange of power for love. Lear has reduced both elements of the monarchy's power and love to personal possessions. His political power is no longer a divine gift for the purpose of his people's governance and protection; it is now an item of negotiability, a piece of land, his private property to dispose of as he wishes. And love is no longer an absolute form of obligation and salvation, but a commodity that can be bartered for land and measured in syllables of flattery. Both the

31. Robert Speaight, "Shakespeare and Politics," p. 17.

power he gives over and the love he seeks in return emanate from nothing within Lear, and yet these must sit well in his accounts, like good bookkeeping. This reduction of political governance and absolute love to mere commodities is what splinters Lear's universe and impels him to ultimate madness. He becomes equal to what at first he so gravely misunderstands: nothing. His retort to Cordelia and to the Fool that "nothing can come of nothing" does not lead to knowledge of self before it is too late.[32]

Lear intends to give his daughters all that is external to himself in exchange for the most internal of all gifts. He wants love in exchange for power when love cannot be rendered except in kind. Cordelia is aware of the impossibility of the exchange, and acts in the only way she can to preserve the love she has for her father in the face of his debasement of terms: she does nothing. She refuses to participate in the exchange, exercising the paradoxical components of salvation in Augustine's City of Man: defenselessness and the strength of self-knowledge. When Lear hopes to threaten her into a more fancy exclamation, with:

> How, how, Cordelia? Mend your speech a little,
> Lest you may mar your fortunes.
>
> (I. i. 94-95)

Cordelia's response only reinforces her distance from any concern for marred fortunes when the truth of her love is in the balance. Lear can only satiate his blind

---

32. Arnold Metzger has written, "We [cannot] say being is the 'counterthrust of nothingness.' On the contrary, its transcendence consists in the fact that this 'substance' has the nothing as its element. It is the elementary, transcendental quality inhering in every existent, which constitutes the categorial order of the universe and at the same time gives the existence that understands itself the constitutive power to master its own finiteness and to be open to its own universe and the universe of things. The nothingness of being is the power that carries man away from himself, that cures him of his nullity. It constitutes man as the subject (self) that cannot become object." "Freedom and Death," p. 240.

indignation and wounded vanity by relinquishing yet
another possession:

> Here I disclaim all my paternal care,
> Propinquity and property of blood,
> And as a stranger to my heart and me
> Hold thee from this for ever.

(I. i. 114-16)

No one can hear these lines in the foreknowledge of *Lear*'s
concluding scenes without wanting to reach out in desperation, somewhat like Kent, to seize the old man by the arm
and bring him to his senses. There is no halting Lear's
desertion, however, and Shakespeare portrays for us with
this first Act's conclusion the ominous theme that accompanies the formation of this new secular nation-state.
Power is assumed in full by those daughters incapable of
love; and the sole source of love, Cordelia, is exiled forever
from the kingdom. In one breathless and extravagant
gesture, Lear has severed love from rule and cast the City
of Man pitilessly into the hands of ruthless power pursued
for its own sake.

Another disturbing political outcome of Lear's tragedy is
that the very questions of succession, legitimacy, and
authority which Shakespeare had raised in the history
plays have all gone sour for us now. There appears to be a
resolute curse at the very core of secular rule, for the
contagion of harm and disease, the gouging of eyes, and
the total deprivation of spirit unto death that issue from
Lear's simple misjudgment seems so disproportionate. That
the frailties of an old man should invite so readily all the
organized cruelties of a new age, that the one emanates so
easily from the other, is the major grief of *Lear*. Not
Richard the Third, Faulconbridge, or Edmund, but Richard the Second, Lear, and Cordelia become the victims of a
freshly polluted universe. These latter feed the new forces
of power in the obliteration of their own legitimacy, their
faith and their love. All that remains is Lear's incomparable
cries at Cordelia's death:

> Thou'lt come no more, Never, never, never, never,
> never . . .
>
> (V. iii. 308-9)

At the end of *Lear,* though the fiercest antagonists have perished along with the better natures, we are given Shakespeare's judgment upon the future, through Edgar:

> The oldest hath borne most; we that are young
> Shall never see so much, nor live so long.

With Lear's torment and death, Shakespeare portrays the unexpected emptiness of secular power. Far from the highest human possession, we must surrender any hope for constructive political action based purely upon it. Albany's farewell makes it all too clear that mere survival will be the new political state's objective:

> Friends of my soul,
> you twain
> Rule in this realm, and the gored state sustain.
>
> (V. iii. 319-21)

From the perspective of Shakespearian tragedy as a whole, it may be difficult to comprehend the complete desolation of *Lear,* which far exceeds that of any of his other works. One cannot make sense of the abdication and all-encompassing void solely on a level of individual crime and punishment. For Lear is not an individual, he is not even a single monarch—he is the ailing symbol of Augustine's governance through absolute love. Similarly, Cordelia is not so much his daughter as that love in essence, the grace of a lost world. When she pleads to the gods on Lear's behalf, it is the plea of one world's nature—its essential humaneness and grace—against its de-naturing by a new world of its own unintended creation:

> O you kind gods,
> Cure this great breech in his abused nature!
> Th' untuned and jarring senses, O, wind up
> Of this child-changed father!
>
> (IV. iii. 14-17)

However the cure might be discovered, we are certain at
Lear's conclusion, through Cordelia's surpassing love, that
it would transcend any political or worldly resolution. In
this instance, we once again turn to John Danby who aids
our comprehension eloquently:

> Shakespeare finds a means to condemn the society he knows is
> historically inevitable. Against it he holds up not only the ideal of
> a transcendent community, but also the needs of a real humanity
> to which the operations of actual society perpetually do violence:
> an idea of unqualified goodness which cannot be measured by
> success in a corrupt society, a goodness more inclusive than that
> covered by the governmental maxims of state expediency.[33]

Danby refers to Cordelia as the "ideal" above, and he later
makes the qualification that Cordelia is not a political or
historical ideal; she is part of a utopian vision that transcends any actual earthly political order.

The nature of this sort of ideal, for Shakespeare, may
render the desolation of *Lear* more accessible to our understanding. He is announcing, in this tragedy, not only the
fate of an inevitable political form but also the corresponding destiny of his own theatre by drawing upon an ideal
that can be found in art alone, as now divorced from its
political association. The nourishing purpose of Shakespeare's tragic theatre, embodying as it did the Globe, had
always been to portray through dramatic art the meaning,
shape, and possibilities of political life. But it is the un-
alterable conclusion of *Lear* that political life has no meaning; it has become nothing but the isolated City of Man, a
world of external appearance and internal emptiness. As
such, his theatre can no longer represent a belief in political
meaning. Instead, it pronounces with *Lear* an end to the
Globe and all that it had symbolized: the theatre of the
world, a hierarchy of religious and political authorities.
Within two years, Shakespeare would move into a private
club, the Blackfriars, and into Lear's world of fantasy:

33. John F. Danby, *Shakespeare's Doctrine of Nature*, p. 101.

> So we'll live,
> And pray, and sing, and tell old tales, and laugh
> At gilded butterflies, and hear poor rogues
> Talk of court news; and we'll talk with them too -
> Who loses and who wins; who's in and who's out -
> And take upon's the mystery of things
> As if we were God's spies; and we'll wear out,
> In a walled prison, packs and sects of great ones
> That ebb and flow by the moon.
>
> (V. iii. 10-18)

Heartsick of bearing action's course in this world, Shakespeare's theatre itself retires as an actor in order to become a more disengaged spectator. And the transvaluation of theatre into mere entertainment at the hands of pandering dramatists is close enough to obfuscate the abyss that remains after Shakespeare's death.

We shall return to the significance of Shakespeare's tragic theatre and the finality of its passage from the Globe to the indoor private stage in the last pages of this Part, but the centrality of *Lear*'s conclusion for the whole bent of Shakespeare's work should be underscored. The experience of tragedy is the acceptance of one's own and one's society's defective judgment and partial (not absolute) sources of measurement for knowledge and action. Tragedy unfolds with an overconfidence in one's own or one's society's vision and power. But the experience of tragedy in the theatre teaches the immensely difficult lesson of seeing that we do not see, that madness is something one can wake up to like the world itself; and that we may not recover except through each other's compassion for our common condition.

The important difference between Shakespeare's theatre and that of Aeschylus lies in what each dramatist derives from the lessons of tragedy. This difference is most lucid in a comparison of *Prometheus Bound* and *Lear*. A curious similarity strikes the spectator in the settings of the solitary cliff in *Prometheus* and the storm scene in *Lear*—

both are cut off from society and from any form of political order. Both Prometheus and Lear find themselves ostracized, punished by the gods disproportionately for their deeds and unable to resume any place in an ordered human life. "Unaccommodated" though they both are, Prometheus is far more resourceful, hopeful and assured even at the height of his rather agonizing plight. Prometheus is young and can withstand the reversals of time, for he knows the outcome of all action: no partial or imperfect vision, however divine, will succeed in maintaining an unjust rule in political life. Prometheus has absolute faith in the forthcoming political resolution of a just polis, ruled by the best leadership. Thus how remote is Lear's world beyond the Realm from that of Prometheus. Lear is too old and beaten by time. He had long deluded himself about some divinely ordered universe, which in his tragedy reveals itself to be no universe at all. Multiple pools of interest and not even the shadow of a great and public recognition can claim his kingdom. As for the future, the political state that would afford governance to this anomic new world would have to hold on, with the ironic resignation of a Hobbes, and learn to make its joyless sojourn through the Kingdom of Darkness.

Lear, in this sense, denotes as well a fundamental departure in the history of tragic theatre. To Aeschylus, theatre had been the educator of the polis. As such, the art form was comfortably in touch with the political form of the city. Whatever vision of reality Aeschylus sought to preserve, he had every assurance of its potential translation into political reality. Shakespeare, however, had to defend the very existence of his theatre against a spiritual banality of the slowly enveloping nation-state. With Shakespeare's last plays, there is a complete loss of confidence in the meaning of political life in its "modern" aspects, and this crisis of confidence cannot help but saturate his tragic art as well. Turning inward, away from Augustine's two cities, reality would now belong to the art itself, as opposed to political life in the world that would always lead to nothing.

This dichotomy between tragic drama and the meaning of political action would persist until the nineteenth and twentieth centuries, when revolutions around the world would rekindle a belief in the constructive potentials of political order and institutions. Many dramatists, notably Brecht, would begin to see that politics and theatre had been similarly stricken by an insufficiency of public life and a malignant growth of individualism, culminating in the unprecedented development of fascist states in the twentieth century. For the time being, however, Shakespeare's *Hamlet* would provide a theory of tragic art in terms of which the medieval state could still preserve formal dramatic existence.

7. The Play Within the Play

Shakespeare's Greek and Roman plays—*Julius Caesar*, 1599; *Troilus and Cressida*, 1602; *Anthony and Cleopatra*, 1606-7; *Timon of Athens*, 1607; and *Coriolanus*, 1608—explore the medieval and Renaissance theories of the state.[1] Renaissance interest in history and political theory was very deeply established, and the pre-social state had been regarded as the sixteenth-century nightmare of chaos.[2] Employing familiar Elizabethan analogies of the beehive, the solar system, and the human body, Shakespeare develops the concept of a "stratified, integrated political society in which all the parts function for the welfare of the whole under the administration of a single, sovereign governor."[3] Of course, analogy had become throughout the Middle Ages "the standard medium for presenting theories relative to the nature and structure of states" and was intended to reveal the true nature of the universe—that "God created every department . . . on the same pattern and subject to the same laws."[4]

Given the hierarchy and interdependence of this universe, the position of central importance was always the governor and all that is germane to his rule. Ulysses' speciality of rule, which has been mentioned, has to do specifically with the task of preserving this complex, hier-

1. Dating is approximate, from the Oxford Edition of Shakespeare.
2. James Emerson Phillips, Jr., *The State in Shakespeare's Greek and Roman Plays*, p. 50.
3. *Ibid.*, pp. 4-5.
4. *Ibid.*, pp. 63, 72.

archical universe in its delicate balance. Only one commander is suited to this task, and the simple lesson of *Julius Caesar* and *Anthony and Cleopatra* is that the society that attempts to overturn monarchical rule will live to regret it. The highest position of power cannot be shared. Shakespeare, like Hobbes and Burke, embraced the fact of inequality among men as necessity in a hierarchical universe. Still, Shakespeare demanded of that universe an inherent charity based upon need; if the polity were well ordered, it would act humanely and compassionately with the grace of a Cordelia. In Augustine's words, Shakespeare would agree that "there could be nothing more fortunate for human affairs than that, by the mercy of God, they who are endowed with true piety of life, if they have the skill for ruling people, should also have the power."[5]

Brutus was an honorable man, but his very virtue, in striving to overtake the seat of power, becomes the more ominous for its determination to shatter the state's order. Whether opposition to the speciality of rule comes from the aristocracy or from the people, Shakespeare never greets it patiently. He envisaged legitimate rebellion against a ruler who himself fails to observe degree in authority. *Coriolanus* and *Troilus and Cressida* afford examples of Shakespeare's judgment upon rulers who fail to uphold degrees of justice required by their own vocation. What mattered, however, was not one part of the political order but its total balance, its continuing existence as a spiritual entity and symbol. It was only the state as an organic and spiritual whole that could sustain the few precious gifts in the City of Man: the illusions of absolute love and beauty, the need for a sense of measure and the resplendent public spectacle. The greatness and mastery of Shakespeare's theatre are at least in part born of his obsession with order as a totality, with his Globe in both senses, even after his

---

5. H. Paolucci, ed., *Political Writings of St. Augustine*, p. 106.

faith in its realization had suffered the fate of Gloucester's eyes.

For the sake of overall balance, Shakespeare is capable of equating slaves and kings in the human condition while simultaneously reserving contempt for angry political masses. "The dominant feature of Shakespeare's plebians, as of all his sons of the people, are stupidity, inconstancy, and cowardliness. They are always blundering, always incapable of any political idea, and impressionable as wax in the hands of their demagogues."[6] Most men, for Shakespeare, are incapable of fulfilling the vocation of rulership, a realization that must have been poorly received by audiences already close to temptations of revolting against monarchical sovereignty.

Coriolanus depicts magnificently the self-oriented polity in which both ruler and ruled shipwreck the political vessel through manipulation and overriding self-interest. The ruler is always foremost a public man for Shakespeare, but Coriolanus attends to his family's private appeals before the needs of state, destroying them both in the process. The curse of democracy in this play is as apparent as it was to Plato. Shakespeare, too, wasted no respect for the body ruling the head. At least there is nobility in Coriolanus' refusal of hypocrisy, but the democratic state resists and is lost along with each man's place in his universe. Shakespeare evinces in these Greek and Roman plays a special interest in articulating the relationships between human character and political order, which Ernest de Selincourt describes as: "the essential relation of the individual to that larger society which is called a nation; and . . . the influences which a man's feelings towards the community have upon his whole life and character."[7] When the proclivity of seventeenth-century audiences was increasingly to

6. Paul Stapfer, *Shakespeare and Classical Antiquity,* quoted in James E. Phillips, Jr., *The State,* p. 153.

7. *From English Poets and the National Ideal,* quoted in Phillips, *The State,* p. 13.

dote on self, Shakespeare seemed determined to portray the social dependency of self. Solely within the hierarchical state could some rare individuals cultivate the semblance of character.

The former heroism of the Trojan and Peloponnesian Wars is strictly bittersweet in Shakespeare's *Troilus and Cressida* and utter apathy in his *Timon of Athens*, reflecting Shakespeare's complete disillusionment with any prospect of war. *Troilus* imbues romantic love with a loyalty that it can no longer claim; and Timon reserves for private friendship that which was once found in the civic polity—generosity and compassion. The conclusions of these two plays are terribly severe: in an ailing or decadent polity, there is no escape save exile or death. One cannot turn for solace to private or romantic enterprises. Timon cannot turn to anyone; his experience of social life has left him with no taste for human company whatsoever. The disintegrating impact of neglected public vocation upon human life within a hierarchical structure is the recurrent theme of these plays.

However, Shakespeare pursues this theme of vocation and degree within a hierarchical state despite his disdain for political remedies within the context of the "gored state" of his historical present. In that context, the vision of state emanating from these last plays, of historical and mythical subject matter, is purely artistic. He is no longer seeking to fulfill a certain specialty of rule in actual politics. That being well behind him now, he is absorbed, in Danby's expression, in the utopian dream of the artist and the good man. That is to say, Shakespeare's devotion to the familiar medieval theory of state, at this point in his career as dramatist, coincides with his development of an "inner play" conception of theatre. Both conceptions seem to confirm his own realizations that theatre could no longer perform its historical task of political education, and that the show of state was no longer great drama. Both theatre and state had become hollow structures in which action could be expansive but never unifying, entertaining but never instructive, and momentarily successful but never exemplary. This represents for Shakespearian tragedy, at the very least, the final emptiness of political power in this world. What this fully means can be more adequately appreciated perhaps when viewed within the framework of Shakespeare's central conception of dramatic art, which is sketched for us in the Player's scene of *Hamlet*. It, in turn, reveals Shakespeare's examination of the state to be different from the representation of a thwarted ideal or melancholy meandering.

The player's scene in *Hamlet* consists of an unprecedented moment in Shakespeare's work when he invites us to sample the tools of his craft and even recreate with him the purpose of his art's vision, or what Susanne Langer calls the "feeling within the form." The essence is given us by Hamlet as he advises the Players before their performance:

> . . . suit the action to the word,
> the word to the action; with this special observance,
> that you o'erstep not the modesty of nature:
> for any thing so overdone is from the purposes
> of playing, whose end, both at the first and
> now, was and is, to hold, as 'twere, the mirror
> up to nature; to show virtue her own feature,
> scorn her own image, and the very age and body
> of the time his form and pressure. Now, this over-
> done, or come tardy off, though it make the
> unskilful laugh, cannot but make the judicious grieve;
> the censure of which one must, in your allowance,
> o'erweigh a whole theatre of others.
>
> (III. ii. 18-31)

There are above all two main aspects of tragic drama's purpose in this passage. The second is more obvious and thus requires less comment—namely, that the "judicious" portion of the audience alone deserves the tragedian's devotion. He does not direct his presentations to just anyone

who crowds the stage, and the critical appraisal of those
who are able to judge is all that matters. The implication
here is *not* that the rest of the audience is so much excess
baggage. Rather the opposite, that the dramatic performance should inspire them with an awareness that far exceeds their own. There can be no compromise between the
provincial and the perceptively critical spectator.

The foremost aspect of the "purpose of playing" from
this passage is "to hold the mirror up to nature." Hamlet
also informs us that this has always been the purpose of
playing, but we know as he speaks that something is missing
from this tidy formulation. We know this, of course,
because Hamlet, who is himself a player in a play, and who
is at the moment absolutely incapable of effecting the
principles of word and action about which he lectures
another group of players, expects these players to accomplish that which is denied him at his initial remove from
"reality." Hamlet tells the players that they must achieve
several objectives through their performances: show virtue
her *feature;* scorn her *image,* and the very age and body of
the time his *form* and *pressure*—a bold assignment when just
moments before, left to himself, he had confessed:

> Had he the motive and cue for passion
> That I have? He would drown the stage
> with Tears.
> And cleave the general ear with horrid speech;
> Make mad the guilty, and appal the free,
> Confound the ignorant . . .
> Yet I, . . .
> Like John-a-dreams, unpregnant of my cause,
> . . . can say nothing;
>
> (II. ii. 571-79)

Why is it, then, that Hamlet believes the players, who lack
his "motive and cue for passion," will be capable of translating word into action where he himself is all but helpless?
The answer is to be found in the very nature of the player's

scene, which constitutes the play within the play. The purpose of action, as Hamlet is aware, can now only be accomplished within that inner play. He is acknowledging in this scene his own life's dependence upon that inner play for revelations he cannot derive without its presentation, and a quality of life perceptible in his very need for the inner play. That quality was a growing rupture in the isolated human city between thought and action and idea and matter. While Hamlet's action might penetrate the darkness of worldly passions, it could not transcend them to overwhelm the otherness of his doubtful spirit. In a world that, rather, makes mad the innocent and conceals the guilty, Hamlet could act only by creating an audience where it would never have voluntarily congregated. Similarly, Shakespeare, late in his career, dramatizes a rational political state better captured by St. Thomas than Augustine before audiences more inclined to pursue religious and economic freedoms than to make sacrifices for the ailing monarchy of James I. But for Shakespeare as later for Hobbes, this political vision was the only one appropriate to a body politic that had lost its soul. Both conceptions—that of the Renaissance state and the inner play—are dramatized not so much to persuade the audiences to adopt some future action but to place them irrevocably before the "facts" and trouble the course of their action in the present.

Throughout the main play, Hamlet's knowledge of his father's murder is never, by any new piece of evidence, fundamentally shaken. But what is clear from the early moment when Hamlet hesitates in responding to his situation is that the fact of murder and his own knowledge of it have nothing to do with reparation through further action. Even though other principal characters in the play cannot be ignorant of the murder, their knowledge seems incapable until the player's scene of forging the inevitable conclusion—that life cannot continue as before, that the bloody deed cannot be undone in further deeds. Hamlet's mind, unable to effect new and fruitful action, has only one alternative—to accept the finality of the appalling act and to force the others to accept it. Only the play within the play—or theatre within a polity cut off from its transcendent meaning—enables men to see their own dilemma of acting in such a bifurcated political and religious universe. Tragic theatre, now symbolically identified as the play within the play, reveals a quality of mind stricken at its creative roots and condemned to a potential sequence of recognition, madness, and death. Jan Kott discusses this element in Shakespeare as the permanent contradiction between values and action, a theme of the twentieth century's theatre of the absurd. In a fundamentally political and secular world, a tragedian can portray a political order as a real alternative only if he believes that action is rational and constructive, that it ultimately relates his mind to the world he knows.

Submerged in this coarse twilight of theatre's relationship to European society and its history, holding the mirror up to nature—as the purpose of tragic theatre—is no longer the Elizabethan presentation of an "exemplar" or perfect pattern, as is assumed for example in "The Mirror of all Christian Kings." The word nature is designed to conjure up the most provocative ambiguities. Meaning both *"natura naturans"* or purposeful man, and also *"natura naturata"* or fallen man,[8] the concept of nature floats, in Shakespeare's formula, between the two without resolution. The purpose of theatre would be now, like that of Hamlet's players, not to reveal a higher meaning in the action, but the source of responsibility for action. When Hamlet tells us that "murder, though it have no tongue, will speak with most miraculous organ" (II. ii. 605), he is expecting that the viewing of a murder by those who are responsible, but not prepared to

8. Virgil K. Whitaker, *The Mirror Up to Nature*, p. 90.

see themselves portrayed upon the stage, will evoke some resistance to the performance. In this conflict between the audience and the play, the former actors, once compelled to become observers of their own acts, will be confronted with the inescapability of their own guilt. This, not revenge and not resurrection, can be the only hopeful response in the isolated City of Man.

The hope lies, as it did when we last spoke of *Lear,* in the recognition of responsibility and its ensuing compassion. In a world of overwhelming economic imperatives, for the first time severing the individual from his community, only the recognition of their own responsibilities could sustain men against their desolation of modernity. With the shattering of the main play, and a transcendent source of reality, whatever keys to the real that remained in the *civitas terrena* would have to be turned through knowledge of self in the reflection of tragic performance. There was no true knowledge to be gained from mere survival in the world. If knowledge had been for Aeschylus and Plato a lifelong journey toward justice, for Shakespeare it is powerless to effect a change in the course of human action. Aeschylus had believed the Athenians could begin anew, but to Shakespeare there remained only the possibility of facing with nobility the various deaths of this world.

8. Theatre as the City of Man

> We remain confronted with the inexplicable fact, or the
> no less inexplicable appearance, of a world travailing
> for perfection, but bringing to birth, together with
> glorious good, an evil which it is able to overcome only
> by self-torture and self-waste.
>
> A. C. Bradley

Even more than previous theatres, those of Elizabethan
and Jacobean England were conspicuously bound to their
cities. These theatres first begin to develop on the very
streets of the city from fourteenth-century *tableaux vivants*
to celebrate the visits of sovereigns. George Kernodle
describes the tableaux as street theatres in which "thousands of people saw represented in paintings or with lay
figures or living actors, popular romantic legends, historical personages, and fanciful allegories. The entry of the
sovereign was a civic ritual of considerable political importance." Between 1370 and 1600, several hundreds of
stationary theatres were constructed with some local varia-
tions in and around London, Antwerp, Paris, and Lyons.[1]
The addition of dialogues and speeches, effecting a transition from painting, tapestry, carved panel, and pantomime
to drama, came in the second quarter of the fifteenth
century, with poets like England's Lydgate, Peele, Jonson,
Middleton, Dekker, and Heywood contributing to the
overall development. When a duke, king, or cardinal

1. G. Kernodle, *From Art to Theatre; Form and Convention in the Renaissance*,
pp. 58-59.

entered the city, "in a sense the whole city, especially the streets along the procession, became a show."[2]

These street theatres honored England's national heroes and Christian and civic virtues upon which its public life was based, evincing a similarity to the beginnings of Greek tragedy from heroic myths and rituals of local villages and tribes.[3] There were principally three types of civic pageantry: outdoor shows for sovereigns on provincial tours (progresses), usually open to the public but held within the private premises of noblemen; royal entries on city streets like the sort described above; and London's Lord Mayor's Show for the Mayor's inauguration each October 29.[4] The same subject matter extended from these pageants to Shakespearian drama, except that the latter stressed plot whereas the processionals largely centered on theme alone. Bergeron speaks of the pageants' themes as celebrating a "victory over the threatening forces, be they national or personal and inward," returning us to the characteristic tensions of all theatre sketched in the first Part.[5] In what follows, we will seek to account for the great theatre movement of Elizabethan and early Jacobean England, suggesting its greater vision and meaning by bringing together different political, cultural, and socio-economic elements, and to discuss the consequences of Shakespeare's participation in a private theatre in his last years.

Frances Yates has shown that the first theatre of the Burbages in England was probably built under the influence of Vitruvius, whose writings had been available in translation by John Dee for at least six years. English adaptations from Roman architecture took on this dimension, according to Yates: "the heavens (the theatre had no ceiling) emphasized and repeated the cosmic plan of the theatre,

2. *Ibid.*, pp. 64-70.

3. William Ridgeway draws a parallel between developments of medieval Christian drama and pre-Greek drama in the celebration of dead heroes through their civic representations; *The Origin of Tragedy*, p. 62.

4. See David M. Bergeron's fine study, *English Civic Pageantry 1558-1642*, p. 3.

5. *Ibid.*, pp. 307-308.

based on the triangulations within the circle of the zodiac; It showed forth clearly that this was a 'Theatre of the World,' in which Man, the Microcosm, was to play his parts within the Macrocosm."[6] She argues that the very architecture of the theatres, inspired and sustained by a vision of cosmic harmony in which the human world found its significance, was in part the source of Shakespeare's unique form of tragedy. Shakespeare's theatre constituted for some twenty-five years what we have called "theatre as the City of Man." This appellation is not unlike Frances Yates' own "theatre of the world," with the exception that the City of Man emphasizes Shakespeare's particular tragic vision. His tragedy assumes the task of enacting upon the stage what the City of Man becomes *in the absence* of the City of God. This is, as I have tried to show, its deepest symbolism. This dramatic envisioning has a specific political reference: the development of the nation-state upon its new "macht" foundations. Shakespeare's tragic theatre documents the ensuing spiritual decomposition that accompanies this new nation-state and its agent, homo-economicus. First, we glimpse the general demoralization and anomie within society; from *Cymbeline* (IV. ii. 14-17), Imogen speaks of it: "society is no comfort to one not sociable. . . . I'll rob none but myself; and let me die, Stealing so poorly." And secondly, the primacy of calculation emerging from the economic changes of the period renders the society as a whole unauthentic in relation to its past. This lack of authenticity is evident in Shakespeare's last plays whose settings of an island and "foreign" removed places only reinforce the alien quality of his own England.

Despite the fact that no explicitly religious theme permeates Shakespeare's theatre to express this alienation, his drama is saturated with moral dilemmas of the sort best

6. *Theatre of the World*, pp. 92-93. Kernodle's *From Art to Theatre*, pp. 110-131, confirms this characteristic symbolism of the Elizabethan theatre as opposed to the other major Renaissance theatre, the Italian "illusionistic." In contrast to the latter, background on the Elizabethan stage never represented a specific locality; it was always symbolic, effecting the symbol of place as opposed to specific location.

captured by Augustine's theory of the *civitas terrena*. Bergeron puts the problem in this way: Renaissance drama for various reasons "surrendered its religious heritage while clinging to the moral tradition."[7] The interpretation of Shakespearian tragedy offered here attempts to shed light on this central complexity in Shakespeare's works by suggesting that his theatre retains Augustine's moral and political perspectives of the human city but without the possibility of its religious salvation. Shakespeare's theatre alone seems to have borne the full transition and tension between a medieval Christian authority and the "modern" era that would bury it.

The London to which Shakespeare had first come was still largely a medieval town, "bounded by a defensive wall, guarded by the Tower, and its center the great cathedral church of St. Paul's." But by 1610, London was already "taking on the airs of a modern city," and the theatre would move more and more to its periphery at a time when the country would become polarized into two parties—Court and Puritans. Under Charles I, theatre would be completely cut off from the growing majority of "sober-minded citizens."[8] The new seventeenth-century dramatists would have no political imperatives of order and community. As we have noted before in this study, tragic theatre suffers the same disintegration as the political order of its origins. England's tragic theatre, born within the setting of the medieval "two cities," is ultimately forsaken, along with the transcendent authority of God's City, for the preferred routine and calculation. After 1610, drama becomes a diversion for a single class, the Court aristocracy.

Finally, theatre as the City of Man is sharply contrasted to the Aeschylean theatre of political memory because it denies the possibility of any political cure for the spiritual decay inherent in the nation-state. The political becomes

7. Bergeron, *English Civic Pageantry*, pp. 7-8.
8. Ashley H. Thorndike, *Shakespeare's Theater*, pp. 25, 423.

the Hobbesian restraining category of order, rather than the former constructive principle of the city. Shakespeare's response to men's turning from God's City is twofold, judging from his last plays: the real test of the City of Man is its courage to see its own delimited nature, and in face of that nature the will to sustain whatever love and beauty might still belong now only to fantasy. Until the last, Shakespeare refused both to construct a vision of rejuvenation or to embrace a logical resignation, "because the evil in man is not matched by a strong enough evil in the nature of the universe of which he is part, because though the balance in favor of the survival of beauty, the increase of understanding, and the rule of law, is very slight, yet the balance tilts that way and not the other."[9]

During the reign of James I, after 1603, public theatres became poor investments for the first time in their brief English history. To account for this turn of events, we will have to retrace two environmental conditions of the Elizabethan theatre's formation and development: the success of European colonial exploitation, and the resulting political and economic changes in seventeenth-century state administration. The first provided capital for experimentation in large public theatres, and the second encouraged a trend to the more easily controlled private stage. Sixteenth-century capitalism exacted a heavy toll for its provisions, not the least of which was the disintegration of the medieval state:

It would be difficult to overestimate the importance of the influx of American gold and silver into Europe in hastening the disintegration of the medieval economic order.... From Spain, mainly by trade ... American gold and silver were diffused throughout the world—particularly to England, France and the Low-Countries.... Between 1500 and 1600, the stock of precious metals in Europe is estimated to have trebled.[10]

9. David Grene, *Reality and the Heroic Pattern; Last Plays of Ibsen, Shakespeare, and Sophocles*, p. 68.

10. L. C. Knights, *Drama and Society in the Age of Jonson*, p. 35.

English investors were quick to seek their fortunes in many public enterprises, including theatres, and the initial response of Elizabethan society seems to have been wonder and awe in face of the dynamic new entrepreneurs. Were there really Edmunds before *Lear*? Consider this portrait of the self-made man from J. Ryder's *Commendations of Yorkshire*, 1588:

They excel the rest in policy and industry, for the use of their trade and grounds, and after the rude and arrogant manner of their wild country they surpass the rest in wisdom and wealth. They despise their old fashions if they hear of a new, more commodious, rather affecting novelties than allied to old ceremonies . . . due commendation hath begun and maintained among the people a natural ardency of new inventions annexed to an unyielding industry.[11]

Like Edmund, these men were not so much diabolical as completely self-centered and ruthlessly efficient. The antinomies between new capitalist enterprise and traditional religious and political orientations soon began to surface, especially over the issue of usury. Bacon had written in his essay "Of Usury" that "ever a state flourisheth where wealth is more evenly spread." The religious premise, of course, urged men not to become rich at the expense of their neighbors, but the rich did indeed add to their wealth and devised arguments in defense of the social polarities they were helping to create: "In 1607, for example, one opinion defended enclosures with the novel argument that 'the good individual is the good general'; while a London pamphleteer of 1616 was prepared to go further still— 'A citizen, however he may be noted for covetousness, and corruption in trading; yet under colour of private enriching himself, he laboureth for the common good.' "[12] In a few years, the dissatisfied social strata would have been

11. Quoted in *ibid.*, pp. 94-95.
12. *Ibid.*, p. 168.

amazed, however, to see the more successful individuals defending their actions on the grounds of a "common good." Private avarice was becoming the national pastime. Thus we are not surprised to discover Jonson's greatest comedy, *Volpone,* playing at the Globe in the same year as *Lear,* and that its "sardonically alert criticism of accumulation is obvious . . . as a manifestation of human greed, peculiarly appropriate in the era that was then beginning."[13]

There are two principal reasons, economic and cultural, for the decline of public theatre after 1600. L. C. Knights suggests that the social and economic factors took full effect only in the early seventeenth century. During the previous two decades, many more men had been educated and trained for prestigious jobs than were available under James I. Long periods of unemployment resulted also from dislocations involved in an intermittent process of modernizing traditional trades from "individual vocations" to mass labor. Some men refused to abandon their former liberty of craft for the crowded and dingy world of the factory and mill. As for the theatre, "Jonson's poverty and Dekker's long imprisonment for debt show how little was to be expected from the stage."[14] A general melancholy fell upon Elizabeth's last years, partly from these economic disillusionments and perhaps mainly from what Donne called the misery that "crucifies the body and mind." The isolation to which we have often alluded steadily enveloped the City of Man, severing it from its transcendent reality, purpose, and meaning, making a mockery of human trust, love, and authority.

The years ahead belonged to Cromwell and Civil War, and to the philosopher of materialist and mechanistic man, Hobbes. Still, Shakespeare's theatre was anachronism long

13. Boris Ford, ed., *Age of Shakespeare,* p. 32.
14. Knights, *Drama and Society,* pp. 200, 201, 324.

before then. The unpopularity of *Lear* when it was first enacted is evidenced in Jonson's own response to it and in the several revised publications of its text, appearing in 1608 and 1609, which deleted the more "unpleasant" encounters and tortures.[15] The Jacobean audiences, in accordance with the times, registered their impatience for the old themes of state legitimacy, authority, and rulership that had been Shakespeare's preoccupation. In place of moral insight, and intellectual honesty, they preferred the soap-operas of Beaumont and Fletcher. Even John Ford (1586-1640), who was the "most delicate stage poet of his time," produced works entitled *The Lover's Melancholy, Tis Pity She's a Whore, The Broken Heart,* and *Love's Sacrifice.*[16]

Government regulation of theatres had begun in 1551 with the licensing of plays, establishing a hierarchy of censorship from King to Privy Council, Lord Chamberlain, and Master of the Revels. With James I, the procedure became highly centralized almost entirely under the Master of the Revels. Censorship was not so much moral as political, forbidding any expression publicly of contempt for authority.[17] The Crown tried to limit the number of playhouses to achieve tighter restrictions over those already in operation, and because officials were always unnerved, during this great theatre period, by threats of sedition, rioting, plague, and fire in the large outdoor, wooden theatres lighted by torches. The Globe's history proved the last fear more than fancy. In 1613, during a performance of Shakespeare's *Henry VIII,* it burned to the ground and was subsequently rebuilt in an octagonal form.[18] But on April 15, 1644, this wondrous theatre was permanently leveled—perhaps a symbol for the ill-fated Stuart monarchy itself.

15. *Ibid.*, p. 315.
16. Ford, ed., *Age of Shakespeare,* p. 425.
17. Thorndike, *Shakespeare's Theatre,* pp. 203-213.
18. *Ibid.*, pp. 55-56.

Shakespeare first composed dramas and began acting in the elder Burbage's original Theater with his company known as the Lord Chamberlain's men. But between 1599 and 1608, Shakespeare's more outstanding and prodigious years, he and the Globe theatre became virtually synonymous. The parallel facts that public theatres were on the wane during his last years, and that the subject matter of his final plays is drastically altered, have much to do with each other and with the same set of circumstances: Shakespeare's move into the private Blackfriars theatre (for all but two months in the summer, which were still devoted to Globe audiences), and his despair of the new decadence in public life. In 1603, the Lord Chamberlain's men, by proclamation of King James I, become the King's men, now identified far more with Court than street audiences; and in 1608, Burbage retrieves his lease to the Blackfriars, transferring the company, including Shakespeare, indoors to the private stage that would now be the center of theatre activity and determine the future course of European drama.[19]

Private Jacobean theatres were distinguished from public theatres in several ways: by charging sufficiently high prices to exclude all but the aristocracy and Court (for example, the Jacobean Court Masques were created especially to flatter the royal image of James I); by smaller and seated audiences, inside roofed and dimly lit playhouses which provided an illusionistic interior for the first time in English theatres; and in general by smaller theatres, which promoted a more confined dramatization and sense of action pertaining almost entirely to private romance or to royal power, and often some combination of the two.

19. *Ibid.*, pp. 304-305, 421. Stephen Orgel, in *The Illusion of Power; Political Theater in the English Renaissance*, has clarified the notion of "private" theatres, insisting that Blackfriars not be included in this category, which properly belongs to Court Masques characterized by an audience that is not selected by the admission box but is rather composed of royalty who are as much a part of the performance as are the actors. See especially pp. 6-8, 43-49.

Importantly, public theatres like the Globe had been built by private producers and were largely conceived and managed by the directors of theatrical companies. Their audiences were drawn on the basis of public interest and amusement and the ability to pay the one penny admission fee. In the private theatres, the concept of the audience drastically changes: the audience of royal spectators produce the Court Masque, so that the private theatres were more the creation of their audiences than the public theatres could ever have been.[20] As early as 1607, Beaumont and Fletcher's *Knight of the Burning Pestle* ridicules the citizen plays and citizen audiences.

It is again not surprising that dramatic subject matters would start to fragment contemporaneously with a split in English society itself, for theatre always expresses the essential aspects of its political culture; thus on the private stage tragedy, history, and romance no longer coexist in the same drama, and each strives rather for its own domain.[21] What Shakespeare felt about these differences between public and private theatres and his own company's commitment to the latter is perhaps best revealed to us in his last plays. Whether he was influenced by Beaumont and Fletcher at this time, as is sometimes alleged, or vice-versa, he had always managed to convey to his audiences, past and present, that among his peers he was no mere company man. With his death, an era of tragic theatre dissolves. George Steiner observes this as "the Great Divide," asserting that the tragic form died in the seventeenth century and that, in Shelley's words, the disappearance of theatre from a nation brings "an extinction of energies which sustain the soul of social life."[22]

We will move on now to conclude this Part with a brief

20. Orgel, *The Illusion of Power*, p. 6.
21. Thorndike, *Shakespeare's Theatre*, pp. 423-426.
22. George Steiner, *The Death of Tragedy*, p. 116.

look at Shakespeare's own closing dramatic compositions. In *Cymbeline, The Winter's Tale,* and *The Tempest,* winter has indeed moved onto Shakespeare's stage, and one senses that the other seasons have relinquished this planet for distant, fertile pastures. The spirit of these plays seems to reach back to Lear's scene in prison with Cordelia: after all the storm and terror had expired from Lear's consciousness, he prefers with Cordelia in his arms to fantasize of a storybook land in which the King's Court is a perpetual enclosure of adventurous news, song, and laughter. This setting of combined horror and fantasy, unmixed, is peculiar to Shakespeare's last plays. Within the confines of fairytale, Shakespeare reflects most bitterly about the real; yet something is retained in these plays, some melancholy optimism that was perhaps most embodied in the figure of Cordelia. There is, however, a transition between *Lear* and these plays, which often verge far more upon farce. Only *The Tempest* observes Shakespeare's former determination, through tragedy, to live in the world and not through the poor surrogates of commodity or voluntary exile.

   Cymbeline, based in part upon the story of Genevra in Boccaccio's *Decameron,* has all the tragic potential of *Othello* with one crucial difference. The husband, once deceived as to his innocent wife's transgressions, orders her to be killed but the command is never really carried out. Afterwards the husband is convinced by a bloody garment that his wife has been duly punished. Through a series of laborious and ludicrous deceptions such as this, the unfortunate pair are at the end reunited; by that time, however, one's responses are numbed. Kenneth Muir argues, to the contrary, that *Cymbeline* is meant to dramatize, in ritualistic fashion, the joy of "redemption and forgiveness."[23] While this can be a persuasive interpretation, it is still quite evident that the real harm—the complete loss of trust—is not obscured but

---

23. K. Muir, *Last Periods of Shakespeare, Racine and Ibsen,* p. 44.

rather underscored by Shakespeare's avoidance of *Othello*'s tragic rhythm, culminating in passion, error, and death.

The good women in these plays take on a suprahuman quality for their very virtue. *The Winter's Tale*'s Hermione, *The Tempest*'s Miranda, and *Cymbeline*'s Imogen are almost untouched by life, steadfastly innocent. Still, Shakespeare is not above juxtaposing side by side this sort of declaration in Cymbeline: "If you buy ladies' flesh at a million a dram, you cannot prevent it from tainting" (I. iv. 135-37). He also provides this description of the moral husband in *Cymbeline:*

> He sits 'mongst men like a descended god:
> He hath a kind of honour sets him off,
> More than a mortal seeming.
>
> (I. vi. 167-69)

But the same husband later in the play has this to say about reality:

> Poor wretches that depend
> On greatness' favour dream as I have done;
> Wake, and find nothing.
>
> (V. iv. 129-31)

When his "gaoler" asks him: "Come, sir, are you ready for death?" He responds, "Over-roasted rather; ready long ago" (V. iv. 153). The virtue of the characters stands as determined fantasy against the horror of the real as it passes alongside unobstructed. *The Winter's Tale* is even more severe in its acrimony. Leontes, who is capable of denying any form of trust, speaks this pathetic insight:

> And many a man there is, even at this present,
> Now while I speak this, holds his wife by th' arm,
> That little thinks she has been sluiced in's absence,
> And his pond fisht by his next neighbor, by
> Sir Smile, his neighbor.
>
> (I. ii. 192-96)

To Leontes, it is a "bawdy planet" where prosperity is the only bond of love (a paraphrase of IV. iii. 575). But it is through the unusual participation of a Chorus called "Time" at the beginning of Act IV that we discover Shakespeare's view on the matter:

> . . . since it is in my power
> To o'erthrow law, and in one self-born hour
> To plant and o'erwhelm custom. Let me pass
> The same I am, ere ancient'st order was,
> Or what is now received: I witness to
> The times that brought them in; so shall I do
> To the freshest things now reigning, and make
> Stale
> The glistening of this present, as my tale
> Now seems to it.
>
> (IV. Prologue)

The only consolation of time's ineluctable ruinations is that just as that bounteous other world was consumed by this spaceless present, so will this present be anathema one day to its own future. Nothing lasts, not even the shallowness and cruelty of one's own age. And there is no mistaking in *The Winter's Tale* the signature of the age: "I see this is the time that the unjust man doth thrive" (IV. iii. 679). *The Winter's Tale* like *Cymbeline* concludes in tiresome reconciliations and "everafters." By providing what his audiences now crave, Shakespeare extracts his dramatic pound. No one could view *The Winter's Tale* and return to his mundane activities of marital life and commerce without the overriding suspicion of every conceivable form of loyalty, friendship, and love.

The Tempest once more returns us to the richer tapestry of *Lear,* in a confrontation of the noble ruling spirit and the bestial underworld of nature, this time in the allegory of Prospero and the island of Caliban. Yet the island, though settled out of injustice and its ensuing tempest, is precluded from tragedy by the excellent governance of Prospero through magic and other supraterrestrial powers. With the assistance of these powers transcendent to purely human and political ones, Shakespeare enables Prospero

to achieve a better fate than Lear. However, the component of magic is absolutely necessary, and it does not in
the end resolve any of the dilemmas of political authority
and justice Shakespeare had so often raised. Caliban, for
example, is restrained by Prospero's powers, but he is
clearly unaffected by the measures of "civil" education
Prospero has assumed with him. He enjoys his retribution
against the "master" in the form of a curse, and it is with
some empathy that one may view his resistance to Prospero's cultural authority in a post-colonial age. More likely
it is Prospero's relationship to Caliban, and not his productive one with Ariel, that most reflects Shakespeare's
final view of the potential influence of political education
upon his own audience at Whitehall.

The Tempest's last scene leaves one to indeterminate spec-
ulations. Miranda and Ferdinand are the inheritors of the
life to come away from the island, but they have no genuine
substance as characters. They approach the beauty and
hope of Cordelia, but they are too gossamer and lack
Cordelia's intricate perception and acceptance of her
father's past. The future will clearly be one without a
history, and Shakespeare deposited little faith in such
beginnings. There is also Prospero's own skepticism; while
willing to leave the island and reenter the world of Milan
that so wronged him in his youth, he must abandon forever his powers and what this implies—an abandonment of
governance. However, there is something vital to be
learned from relinquishing the island and returning to the
world, something we all can recognize as an acceptance of
the imperfections of this world where we must enact our
destinies; and Shakespeare did not even in the end depart
from this acceptance of the only human stage despite its
ironic inadequacies and disillusionments. A certain passage of Augustine's comes to mind in this last scene, one
that describes even the wise in the City of Man:

In the city of the world both the rulers themselves and the people they dominate are dominated by the lust for domination. . . . The one city loves its leaders as symbols of its own strength. The other says to its God: "I love thee, O Lord, my strength." Hence, even the wise men in the city of man live according to man, and . . . become vain in their reasonings, and their senseless minds have been darkened.[24]

Like Prospero, we too being human should not be contented with a lust for domination that darkens the mind, but should seek some form of association in life that will be bonded through friendship and love. In these last plays, we are forced to embrace a final separation between the cold shabbiness of the new political and economic world and community ideals reserved for the lyrical fantasy or poem. Thus, a dual vision is what Shakespeare emphasizes toward the end. The art of that vision is to reveal the self both as isolated from the island-city of love it seeks *and* as a dependent part of a new political universe, retaining the tensions that have made his theatre possible. This vision was particularly pertinent to a society whose Adam Smith, Ricardo, and John Stuart Mill would eventually draw the very contours of liberty around the solitary and non-conforming individual. By that time, theatre as a public institution would no longer have substance in the languishing publics of Europe.

24. *City of God*, XIV, 28.

III. Reconstruction: Brecht and Marx

9. Reconstituting the Audience

Today it is altogether doubtful how far the spirit of
modern nations can be judged by the need they feel for
an objective, ideal picture of life presented on the stage.

Jacob Burckhardt, *Force and Freedom*

European theatre from the late seventeenth century
until the end of the eighteenth century is known generally
as middle-class drama; and this in itself suggests the origin
of what Fergusson has called the fragmentation of our own
contemporary theaters.[1] For it is during this period, and
even throughout the late nineteenth-century "realist" reaction to it, that the audience consistently decomposes. In
English, French, and German theatres, audiences were
drawn primarily from one social class, the bourgeoisie, and
the plays were for the most part thematically confined to a
dramatization of benign human nature and its chance
catastrophes. In relation to the fundamental meaning of
theatre as audience,[2] middle-class drama went a long way
toward eliminating the art form in Europe altogether, first
by shattering its wider public participation and second by
reducing its dramatic content to what has been called "the
calm haven of secure and honored respectability."[3]

Nolte locates the beginnings of middle-class drama in the
late Elizabethan period with its "spread of sentimentalism,
the rise of journalism, and the dissemination of popular

1. F. Fergusson, *The Idea of a Theater*, pp. 237-239.
2. Elaborated in Part I above.
3. Fred Otto Nolte, *The Early Middle-Class Drama (1696-1774)*, p. 132.

propaganda."[4] George Lillo's *Fatal Curiosity*, considered to be the first "bourgeois" tragedy, and Lessing's *Miss Sara Sampson*, for example, portray an absence of class prejudice and a placid acceptance of society and its comforts, presenting action itself as a poor substitute for leisure and passivity. "The worthy citizens who formed the bulk of theatrical audiences and who came to the playhouse to be mildly moved and agreeably refreshed" were never disturbed by corcuscating insights.[5] One of its own composers, the French playwright Saurin, anticipated this drama's future course in his Preface to *Beverly* in 1770. Long after the distinguished theatre of Moliere had expired, he writes: "The bourgeois tragedy is a new field which, cultivated by hands more skilful than my own, may yield a few happy harvests. I say a few harvests, for this type is confined between two almost inevitable reefs: low rascality and exaggerated fictitiousness."[6]

As the theatre audience loses contact with the larger society, public attention turns to the psychological novel which also emerges in the eighteenth century and, as Nolte aptly remarks, far outstrips drama for conveying "the low drone of daily existence."[7] Against this background of a stultifying middle-class drama and competition with the novel, the manifold expressions of "realist" theatre begin to take shape, first in the romantic tradition against which it later rebels. The latter part of the eighteenth century constitutes an important transition in this respect, as the Sturm and Drang dramatists oppose their "inner form" conception of drama to the previous neoclassicism which would continue to dominate the French stage even after its Revolution and subsequent Napoleonic rule. Only Victor Hugo in 1830 would begin to draw from the German romantic tradition's more flexible dramatic form within which theatre might recover from its "repose of illusion,"

4. *Ibid.*, pp. 93-94. 6. *Ibid.*, p. 145.
5. *Ibid.*, p. 204. 7. *Ibid.*, p. 211.

returning to serious interpretations of human action and political life once again.[8]

The various movements toward realist drama were concerned with a more accurate representation of the "real world" than had ever been possible in bourgeois tragedy and neoclassicism, and the pursuit of this objective tended to underscore the significance of environment for the meaning of human action. "More real" begins to be interpreted as: "more realistically recreated." Thus, the realist stage attempts to give spectators an actual location with moveable props, furniture, and pictorial detail. By 1875, this stage is characterized by two principal elements: illusionism (which we recall from the Italian Renaissance stage) or the illusion of reality on the stage, and the theatre as the reproduction of a specific environment.[9] The first element ironically leads to what is known as the fourth-wall convention," undermining the development of European theatre even more than its eighteenth-century precedents by regarding the audience as simply nonexistent. Actors must treat the open stage as a fourth wall, never betraying any awareness of being observed and protecting at all costs the spectator's oblivion. A theatre experience that had once historically constituted a collective memory would now reinforce, by dramatic convention, private forgetfulness. Once again, and this time decisively, the theatre finds its natural rival outside the dramatic arts: in 1910 D. W. Griffith releases his film "The Birth of a Nation" and permits the uninvolved spectator to experience a complete divorce from living actors.[10] Only Brecht, in the early 1920s, seems to have perceived that the very existence of theatre depended entirely on reconstituting the audience by breaking down the fourth-wall convention (retained even by Shaw) and once more expanding the

8. See John Gassner, *Form and Idea in Modern Theatre*, pp. 7-10.
9. *Ibid.*, pp. 18-19.
10. *Ibid.*, p. 62.

audience across class distinctions to its entire polity. For
these tasks, he would turn to eastern forms of drama for
inspiration.[11]

The second aspect of the realist stage, its emphasis on
environment, was more hopeful for repairing the breach
between theatre and society—a breach that characterized
the relationship between state and society as well. With
increasing industrialization and institutionalization of
European and American nations in the nineteenth century,
the state like its theatre counterpart grew more and more
estranged from its flesh and blood constituencies. Pioneer
realist dramatists, especially in Scandinavia and Russia,
took cognizance of these political and dramatic rifts, their
themes reflecting an age of democratic revolutions that had
reawakened in European consciousness dilemmas of
liberty in terms of social and economic inequities. Emile
Zola in 1873 asserts for the first time since Shakespeare that
"modern" drama should explore "the twofold life of the
character and its environment," and Antoine's Theatre
Libre in 1887 reinforces the notion that dramatic characters should be specifically occupied with material realities
in a material world."[12] The first outstanding exploration of
the political setting and its conflicts, however, is achieved in
Ibsen's *An Enemy of the People.*

Shaw recognized Ibsen's work as a key juncture between
bourgeois theatre and his own contemporary realist perspective, primarily for the closing scene of *A Doll's House*
(considered "obscene" in its day) in which husband and
wife sit down to discuss their marriage. Up to that point,
Shaw insisted, the play would have merely echoed two cen-

11. In India, Ceylon, Burma, Bali, Java, Japan, and China the audiences are
totally involved in experiences of theatre; audiences in the Orient "consider the
theater a place to live, not a place to sit." See Pronko, *Theater East and West,* pp.
179ff; and John Willett, ed. and trans., *Brecht on Theater,* "Alienation Effects in
Chinese Acting," pp. 91-99.

12. Gassner, *Form and Idea,* p. 21. Diderot and Montesquieu had treated this
theme in other contexts, of course.

turies of dismal domesticities on the stage. But suddenly with the reappearance of discussion (reaching back to Aeschylus' *Prometheus*), the theatre claims a new life. Arthur Miller describes Ibsen's achievement in ways that also remind us of the Greek theatre's beginnings, referring to Ibsen as "one who 'squeezed out' the 'hidden connections' of events to the mores, habits, and social institutions of the time—so that a tension, a contradiction immediately appeared."[13] After Ibsen, playwrights persisted in their efforts to dramatize discussion and social and political settings with greater authenticity and clarity. By 1902, Strindberg spares us no delusions in his *The Dance of Death*, in which an extreme "naturalism" translates Ibsen's sudden domestic upheaval into a couple's ceaseless mutual laceration.

In the same year, Chekhov takes the realist stage to the Russian provinces while Gorki explores the urban slums. Stanislavski's Moscow Art Theatre at this time attempted to satisfy the realists' every passion for exact replica in costume and stage production. One writer reminisces that during a performance of Chekhov's *The Cherry Orchard*, "the spectators can detect the genuine aroma of fresh ripe cherries," and that Madame Chekhov attempted to "live" herself into the part of Natasha in Gorki's *The Lower Depths* by rooming with a prostitute.[14] This latter play, preceding the Russian Revolution by only fifteen years, nearly provoked an uprising within Moscow's larger public, and police finally surrounded the Art Theatre in order to prevent a "revolutionary outburst." In fact during the early decades of the twentieth century, theatre becomes increasingly associated with revolutionary movements, and playwrights are caught up in newborn commitments to political change and constructing new political orders. States and theatres begin to reverberate once again not only with a

13. *Ibid.*, pp. 45, 66.
14. *Ibid.*, pp. 23-38.

heightened sense of action but with a belief in its more
sanguine possibilities.

Thus in 1899, the Theatre of Dublin is established out of
the Irish Nationalist Movement to nourish the Irish intelligentsia; by 1925, O'Casey's *The Plough and the Stars* is still
accompanied by political demonstrations.[15] Influenced by
Moscow's Art Theatre, the Tsukiji Little Theatre opens in
Japan in 1924, intending to dramatize among other things
principles of communism.[16] Radical theatre groups abound
in Paris, Berlin, and New York. In Burma, a traditional
relationship between the stage and politics ends in catastrophe by the latter part of the nineteenth century. This
country's most significant dramatist, U Pon Nya, had
written *Wizaya* to support an attempted coup by a contemporary prince. The very success of the play persuades
the ruling elite to prepare sufficient opposition to crush the
revolutionary group, and both prince and playwright are
finally executed.[17] In China, the Peking Opera becomes
even more central to political culture after the Revolution;
and India's Mahrashtrian theatre bitterly denouces British
colonialism in its historical drama, *Bhau Bandki,* written
over one hundred years ago.[18] Although these instances
barely touch upon the relationships between revolution
and theatre, it is important to note that they exist, continue
to be fundamental in recent world theatre activity, and that
from an international perspective theatre that is *not* political is the exception rather than the rule.

Returning to early twentieth century realist theatres, we
can locate one of Brecht's and Piscator's closest precursors
in Russia one year after its Revolution. The composer-
director Meyerhold begins to dramatize the "collectivist

15. *Ibid.,* p. 82.
16. Faubion Bowers, *Theatre in the East; A Survey of Asian Dance and Drama,*
p. 349.
17. *Ibid.,* p. 112.
18. *Ibid.,* pp. 62, 273-281.

aims and the industrialization of society along with a depersonalization of the individual."[19] It is this sort of vision that first informs Brecht's work, but even more important than his dramatic themes are his new dramatic purposes. For Brecht sees clearly the historical identifications of theatres and polities, and with respect to this he understands the failings of realism. From Brecht's perspective, the following purposes or tasks for drama have become essential. First, to reconstitute the audience as inclusive not only of its own society's social and economic classes but of the classes of other societies as well. The democratic and communist revolutions whose epilogues were World Wars had penetrated forever the absolute boundaries of sovereign nations, and a theatre could no longer be parochial and hope to survive.[20] Second, theatre had also to expand its sense of action. Realism, especially after Freud, creatively revived tensions of consciousness and the unconscious, but Brecht would proceed to build upon the tensions of self and community and religion and politics within his own dramatic forms, which combined comedy, tragedy, and opera. Third and finally, theatre had to go beyond realism to provide openness and flexibility in dramatic style and theatre architecture. For this purpose, Brecht drew much of his material from Japan and China, whose dramas, influenced by classical Indian dance and drama, provide an astonishing array of theatre delights and cultural enrichment.

When Brecht began writing for theatre during World

19. Gassner, *Form and Idea*, p. 196.

20. The new requisites for theatre recalled the theme of Aeschylus' *The Persians*, in which an enemy country could be sympathetically portrayed in a state's national drama. Arthur Miller's *Incident at Vichy* is an excellent post-World War II example of this worthy approach to theatre. As will be evident later, however, this expansion of audience identity beyond societal borders began to bear, over time, the costs of fierce and chaotic international developments, culminating eventually in the problematical displacements of playwrights and their temporary theatres in Europe and America.

War I, there were largely three centers for experimental drama: Moscow, Berlin, and New York. And though Europe is in general by the late nineteenth century well seeded with what Brecht indignantly refers to as "culinary theaters" (where the stomach is well-fed and the head empty),[21] Germany alone, Brecht felt, should be the logical center for an enduring reconstruction of theatre.[22] Between 1918 and 1932, he wrote: "At present it's Germany, the home of philosophy, that is leading in the large-scale development of the theater and the drama. The theater's future is philosophical."[23] What Brecht means by "philosophical" draws much of its weight from Hegel and Marx. He constructs a theory of theatre in relation to social change which we will see him continue to develop over his creative years. Perhaps he best stated it later in his life, between 1947 and 1948:

We need a type of theatre which not only releases the feelings, insights, and impulses possible within the particular historical field of human relations in which the action takes place, but employs and encourages those thoughts and feelings which help transform the field itself. . . . The field has to be defined in historically relative terms. In other words, we must drop our habit of taking the different social structures of past periods, then stripping them of everything that makes them different; so that they all look more or less like our own, which then acquires from this process a certain air of having been there all along, in other words of permanence pure and simple. Instead we must leave them their distinguishing marks and keep their impermanence always before our eyes, so that our own period can be seen to be impermanent too.[24]

21. See Willett, *Brecht on Theater*, pp. 27, 39-42, 52, 87-89.

22. Subsequent events proved this a lamentable statement, but the belief in a single nation's central importance for theatre continues. In 1956, Japan's distinguished actor-director, Senda Koreya, said: "In the sixteenth century England had Shakespeare. The seventeenth century saw France's greatest dramas. The eighteenth century was German and the nineteenth Russian. The twentieth century . . . belongs to Japan's modern theatre of tomorrow," in Bowers, *Theatre in the East*, p. 360.

23. Willett, *Brecht on Theater*, p. 24.

24. *Ibid.*, p. 190.

As with Aeschylus and Shakespeare, Brecht's theories of history, society, and theatre are interdependent, but the world had undergone enormous change between 1600 and 1900. The crucial difference between Brecht and Shakespeare, and the difference that recalls Aeschylean tragedy to the forefront once again, is that for Brecht change is a positive phenomenon characterizing all life and denoting constructive human potential. This is no naive formula on his part. It is not even straightforwardly Marxian, because Brecht maintained this view in a lifetime that coincided with genocide, the atom bomb on Hiroshima, and continuing fascism, all developments that do not rhapsodize scientific progress and productive humanity. His Galileo is made to describe a new age as "blood-spattered whores" (scene 13); and still Brecht insists: "The theater becomes a place for philosophers, and for such philosophers as not only wish to explain the world but wish to change it."[25]

We find in Brecht a more self-conscious dramatist than we have encountered before. During his lifetime, he wrote voluminous notes and essays on the purpose of his art and work. Instead of interpreting one scene in *Hamlet* to derive Shakespeare's sense of purpose and meaning in theatre, we have Brecht's own theory of the Epic theatre. Because Brecht detested the romantic image of the struggling poet alone and outcast, which he associated with Goethe, he preferred to work openly in groups, to encourage wide criticism and reworking of his plays, and to borrow unashamedly from many international sources of theatre. We have seen how Aeschylus was influenced by the philosophies of Solon and Heraclitus, and that Shakespeare's work reveals the imprint of an Augustinian universe. With Brecht we have a written acknowledgement reiterating the subtle relationships between a concept of the theatre and its correlative vision of the political and spiritual universe.

It is known that Brecht's earlier plays, like *Baal* and *In the*

25. *Ibid.*, p. 80.

Swamp, are attempts at some sort of realism but do not capture the more coherent political themes of his work as a whole. He explains his original orientation in a distinction between poetry and theatre: "My poetry is more private. . . . In my plays I don't just give my own private mood, but also the whole world's. In other words, an objective view of the business, the opposite of mood in the usual poetic sense."[26]

Brecht began reading *Das Kapital* in 1926, and he describes Marx's influence upon his conception of the theatre in this note: "When I read Marx's *Capital* I understood my plays. . . . It wasn't of course that I found I had unconsciously written a whole pile of Marxist plays; but this man Marx was the only spectator for my plays I'd ever come across. For a man with interests like his must of necessity be interested in my plays, not because they are so intelligent but because he is—they are something for him to think about."[27]

This self-reflection of Brecht's is instructive, especially for those who would criticize his dramas strictly in terms of his political positions and who overlook his fundamental humor, evident in the previous quotation. Brecht's particular expression of Marxian themes made him as suspect to the International Communist Party as it did to Americans. The Soviets criticized his severe representation of party discipline in *The Measures Taken* (1930), and Americans frustrated Brecht's efforts to dramatize political realities emanating from this country's policies of the 1940s and early 1950s.

Although Brecht's theatre is inspired both in form and substance by political theories drawn mainly from Marx and Lenin, theory is meant to serve the theatre in its role as political educator and not as an ideological weapon. Brecht makes this point when discussing the revolutionary Berlin theatre of Piscator in the early 1920s: "The breakdown of

26. *Ibid.,* p. 14.   27. *Ibid.,* pp. 23-24.

this eminently political theater must be attributed to political causes. The increase in the theater's value as political education clashed with the growth of political reaction."[28] The fact at that time obvious to Brecht also drew our attention at the outset of this study, that theatre is created as the critical expression of a given political order's meaning and destiny. In adopting Marx's explanation of social change through class conflict, Brecht argues along other lines as well that there is no such thing as an apolitical theatre: "Society cannot share a common communication system so long as it is split into warring classes. Thus for art to be 'unpolitical' means only to ally itself with the 'ruling' group . . . the choice of viewpoint is also a major element of the actor's art, and it has to be decided outside the theater. Like the transformation of nature, that of society is a liberating act; and it is the joys of liberation which the theater of a scientific age has got to convey."[29]

Throughout his career, Brecht's work reflected his determination to convey the need for liberation in the theatres of a scientific age, but many audiences remain hostile to his gestures, finding his theatre either too threatening or too crude. Brecht's dilemma was then two-fold: how to reintroduce the *problem* of liberation among peoples who feel they have nothing more to learn about freedom; and how to devise a theatre in which the ancient functions of recollecting and seeing would once again be performed by the audience. In order to understand Brecht's approach to theatre, in light of these problems, we will discuss seven of his plays, ranging from pre-Nazi Germany, to Brecht's exile in America and his return to East Germany in the 1950s. These plays reflect an international context issuing from the Second World War and his theory of the Epic theatre, which is developed and revised in light of Brecht's own experiences as a dramatist and critical observer of political life.

28. *Ibid.*, p. 130.   29. *Ibid.*, p. 196.

10. Reclaiming the State

You are finished, statesman
The State is not finished.
Allow us to change it
According to the conditions of our lives.
                                        Brecht,
                            Lindbergh's Flight, 1930

Brecht first addressed himself to the fact that few theatres since Shakespeare had been able to speak for and attempt to educate their societies as a whole. Shakespearian drama, encompassing the broadest possible thematic territory—political, spiritual and psychological—had centered on monarchical rule and his age's unique shift of state from medieval foundations to its emergence as an empire-building enterprise. Theatres of realism had ultimately shown that contemporary drama could no longer devote its energies to the woes of monarchy in neoclassical plays at a time when the industrial nation was being firmly established in Europe, America, and Japan. But Brecht contributed the only dramatic focus which was capable of comparison with Shakespeare's imposing breadth, and which was even more appropriate, on a worldwide level perhaps, to the splintered universe of our own century.

As Shakespeare drew his essential tragic vision from a passing monarchy, Brecht derives his own from the democratic polity torn by the ideological appeals of fascism and socialism. Specifically, Brecht understood that his own drama could only be as meaningful and sensitive as Shakespeare's was to the central issues of his day if it embodied a critique of the democratic polity, articulating democracy's diverse potentials for despotism and the nation-state's new social and economic bases of power. Brecht above all portrays the contemporary state in Weber's sense, as ruled through bureaucratic administration, and here his work transcends its Marxist orientation and any simple identification with communism. The two institutions, the army and the factory, which most typify the early twentieth-century state's new bases of power and its routinization provide the contexts for two of his most provocative plays: *A Man's A Man* (1926) and *Saint Joan of the Stockyards* (1929-1930). Like many other writers, Brecht is drawn to Marx's view of history, institutions, and class not from the pristine euphoria of another political perspective but from an over-riding detestation of the great World War, its grief and inexplicable destruction of human life.

When the problem of political leadership in Shakespeare was last raised, we discovered that with *Henry V*, he abandons the "modern" state to a kingship of professional and calculating administrators. In Brecht's plays, which are saturated with political themes, there are far fewer explorations of political leaders (with the important exceptions of his experimental adaptations of Marlowe's *Edward II* and Shakespeare's *Coriolanus*). Brecht gives us mercenary soldiers in India, a Chinese prostitute, a Russian peasant woman, a scientist, a social reformer, an itinerant trader, and others. What has happened to the great theme in tragedy of political leadership? The answer can be traced to the very routinization of leadership within the nation-state; of course, we turn to Weber for the description:

In a modern state the actual ruler is necessarily and unavoidably the bureaucracy, since power is exercised neither through parliamentary speeches nor monarchical enunciations but through the routines of administration. . . . The democratic state no less than the absolute state eliminates administration by feudal, patrimonial, patrician or other notables holding office in honorary or hereditary fashion, in favor of employed civil servants. . . . The modern mass army, too, is a bureaucratic army, and the officer is a special type of official, distinct from the knight, the *condottiere,* the chieftain, or the Homeric hero. . . . Sociologically speaking, the modern state is an "enterprise" (*Betrieb*) just like a factory: This exactly is its historical peculiarity. . . . Increasing public ownership in the economic sphere today unavoidably means increasing bureaucratization.[1]

Brecht explores the military dimension of state in *A Man's A Man,* which he calls "a comedy with songs." As in the viewing of many Chaplin films, we laugh throughout Brecht's play until at last we realize it has told the simple story of a man who loses his identity and is happier for his anonymity. The second or third time one sees Chaplin or Brecht, it is less easy to merely laugh. The Prologue prepares us with these words; this is "the story of Galy Gay, a homey sort of fellow, a loyal and loving husband, but transformed, nay transfigured, at last, into a citizen, a patriot, a soldier, and builder of empire." The transfiguration is performed by three soldiers of the British colonial army in Tibet, Afghanistan, and Burma. Their fourth buddy has deserted, and they need a replacement. Galy Gay is perfect for their needs, because of his flawless capacity for never saying no. We come across this quality again in Brecht's *Good Woman of Setzuan.* It is for Brecht a prerequisite for efficient bureaucratic institutions and the maintenance of a corrupt social order. Willful character has no place in the mass society where human beings are interchangeable like parts of a machine. *A Man's A Man* declares that men are indeed interchangeable, and that many men find this preferable to initiative, loyalty, and individuality.

Brecht keeps before us the element of transfiguration. Galy Gay is at first an ineffectual simpleton, but he evinces this sort of sensitivity:

1. *Economy and Society, Vol. III,* (eds.) Guenther Roth and Claus Wittich, Bedminster Press, New York, 1968, pp. 1393-94.

I've often had enough of a fish before I've ever seen it. But some people have their fish many times over. They go to buy it, then they do buy it, then they carry it home, then they cook it to a turn, then they wolf it down, and even then, when they're in bed at night, and think they have written finis to the chapter entitled Digestion, that sad little fish is still keeping them busy. All because they have no imagination. (3rd number.)

By the last scene, we see the margin of difference as Galy Gay has become the "Human Fighting Machine." His greatest self-declaration is: "I am the man who single-handed has taken the Sir el Jowr mountain fortress. . . . I believe one man's as good as another." The contempt for individuality is also remarkably embodied in the figure of Bloody Five, the hero of the colonial army. His name is attributed to his execution of five Hindu men, whom he killed at close range for the purpose of testing his rifle's firing power. The sole inhibition upon his readiness to blast "the enemy" is a sexual one. His reputation for being undefeated in war is always at the mercy of petty sexual betrayals of manhood. Finally, he settles his self-conflict and fear by castrating himself, exclaiming: "I hereby assume my responsibilities. I must—to remain Bloody Five." (10th number.)

In the lives of both Galy Gay and Bloody Five, the military eliminates competing forms of identity. Galy Gay is willing to dissolve his past along with his name in order to have security and acceptance; Bloody Five regards the potency of killing other men far more essential to his identity than sexual conquest. Brecht writes of his intention in this play:

It does not make the hero the victim of an inevitable fate, nor does it wish to make the spectator the victim, so to speak, of a hypnotic experience in the theater. In fact, it has as a purpose the "teaching" of the spectator a certain quite practical attitude; we have to make it possible for him to take a critical attitude while he is in the theater. . . . Human behavior is shown as alterable; man himself as dependent on certain political and economic factors and at the same time as capable of altering them.[2]

This characteristically Marxian theme is given significant exploration in *St. Joan of the Stockyards,* which is set in a Chicago meat-packing plant during the Depression. While this play is a parody of Schiller's *Maid of Orleans* and borrows from Shaw's *St. Joan,* it is clearly an original work. For its sheer starkness, depth of humor, and excellent dialogue, it is Brecht's most impressive early drama. Long after the particular contexts of colonial armies and pre-union factory oppression are removed from political life, the more profound aspects of alienation that are the legacies of these contexts continue to upset Brechtian audiences.

Joan Dark represents the Black Straw Hats, a version of the Salvation Army, and begins her task of social reform from the perspective of compassion for the poor and criticism of their abysmal working conditions. She proceeds directly to Pierpont Mauler, the infamous millionaire owner of the stockyards, whom Joan recognizes because he has "the bloodiest face" (scene 3).[3] He directs her, at first through his assistant, to view the internal operations of the plant so that she might better comprehend the "nature" of the people she is defending.

Scene 4, entitled "The Broker Sullivan Slift Shows Joan Dark the Wickedness of the Poor," demonstrates the insensitivities of the poor even in the face of death in their own families. A Mr. Luckerniddle has accidentally fallen into the meat-grinding machine and come out as a "meatloaf." After several days, when his wife appears at the factory in search of her husband, Joan anticipates her indignation, outrage, and grief. The factory tells her that her husband probably took off for San Francisco. Mrs. Luckerniddle rejects this alibi, insisting that she cannot support herself without her husband. The factory then offers her twenty

2. Willett, *Brecht on Theater,* pp. 78, 86.
3. In Eric Bentley, tr., *Seven Plays by Bertolt Brecht,* p. 167.

free dinners to forget about the whole thing; she gloomily accepts, returning to wolf down the meals night after night. Joan, horrified, pleads with Mrs. Luckerniddle, "Won't you wait until tomorrow? If you give up your husband now, no one will ask after him any more." But the woman responds, beginning to eat greedily, "He's gone to Frisco."

Joan continues to see incidents of total selfishness and cruelty in the factory. Her conclusion, however, is this: "If their wickedness is beyond measure, then so is their poverty. Not the wickedness of the poor Have you shown me, but *the poverty of the poor*. . . . O thoughtless rumor, that the poor are base! You shall be silenced by their stricken face!" This scene recalls Marx's words: "Thus all passions and activities must be submerged in *avarice*. The worker must have just what is necessary for him to want to live, and he must want to live only in order to have this."[4]

The play continues to undercut the pre-Marxist assumptions of rugged individualism—that poverty is the result of human nature rather than the creator of it—in order to enact the essential truth for Brecht and Marx: "Life is not determined by consciousness, but consciousness by life."[5] Joan's first political realizations are followed by a realization that religion is a partner in oppression rather than a genuine consolation of the spirit. When Mauler fails to reopen the factory after repeated promises and a week of starving his workers in the snow outside the plant, Joan tries once again to persuade him to think of the workers. He responds by urging her to return to her true vocation in religious work:

> In a word, you really ought
> To set God up once more—
> The only salvation—and
> Beat the drum for Him so that He may
> Gain a foothold in the regions of misery and His
> Voice may ring out among the slaughterhouses.
>
>   (scene 8)

4. T. B. Bottomore, tr. and ed., *Karl Marx, Early Writings*, p. 172.
5. Marx and Engels, *The German Ideology*, in Feuer, ed., *Marx and Engels*, p. 247.

Joan replies:

> I know I should be overjoyed to hear
> That God is going to be helped, only
> I belong to those for whom
> This does not mean real help. And to whom
> Nothing is offered. . . .
>
> (scene 8)

By the end of the play, Joan will add:

> Therefore, anyone down
> here who says there is a God
> where none can be seen,
> A God who can be invisible and yet help them,
> Should have his head knocked on the pavement
> Until he croaks.
>
> (scene 11)

God, like officially sanctioned morality, is only the comfort of luxury that needs no comfort. When Joan dies of pneumonia at the age of 25, striking with the snowbound workers, both Mauler and the Black Straw Hats martyrize her death in order to conceal the fact that she died in determination to overthrow the factory's structure of power. Brecht reminds us of this theme in Marx and Engels' *German Ideology*: "For the mass of men, i.e., the proletariat, these theoretical notions do not exist and hence do not require to be dissolved, and if this mass ever had any theoretical notions, e.g., religion, etc., these have now long been dissolved by circumstances."[6] Before she dies, Joan gives us a Brechtian metaphor of society as the "seesaw," the vision that has necessitated her revolutionary action. For fear of death cannot surpass the pain of a perpetually dehumanized existence nor the logic of what she sees:

> I see this system and on the surface
> It has long been familiar to me, but not
> In its inner meaning! Some, a few, sit up above
> And many down below and the ones on top

6. *Ibid.*, p. 260.

Shout down: 'Come on up, then we'll all
Be on top,' but if you look closely you'll see
Something hidden between the ones on top and
    the ones below . . .
It's a plank and now you can see it quite clearly,
It is a seesaw, this whole system. . . .
(scene 9)

With the 1930s and its progress toward fascism in Germany, Brecht transports his purely Marxist concerns into the twisted framework of an emerging totalitarian politics. Between 1932 and 1934, he writes *The Roundheads and the Peakheads,* but it is first performed only in Copenhagen in 1936.[7] Thus, we begin to discover what becomes a characteristic feature of much contemporary drama: the playwright must often export his plays about the world; he does not have a home city as Aeschylus and Shakespeare did, and attachment to the theatre, afloat in many nations, may mean near-permanent exile from the country of his birth and no political freedom elsewhere. *The Roundheads and the Peakheads* satirizes Hitler's racial theories, exposing the issue of race as a camouflage for the real issues of poverty and communism. Brecht demonstrates, as well, the nation-state's excellent capacity for banal demagoguery. Between 1935 and 1938, he continues his exposure of Hitler with *Furcht und Elend des Dritten Reiches,* translated in 1945 as *The Private Life of the Master Race.* First performed in Paris in 1938,[8] it proceeds through 28 scenes to describe the horror of the concentration camps, the anti-fascist efforts of the communist underground movement, anti-Semitism, and cases of personal and familial betrayal within fascist society.

Although Brecht composes various works during the decade of the 1930s, including *Senora Carrar's Rifles* (1937) treating the Spanish Civil War, it is his unusual piece *Mother Courage* (1939) that best dramatizes what Brecht expected the world's nations would learn from their experiences of

7. Martin Esslin, *Brecht: The Man and His Work,* p. 306.
8. *Ibid.,* p. 308.

fascism. As we have seen, the nation-state is aptly represented, for Brecht, by its two major institutions, the military
and industry. In *Mother Courage*, Brecht depicts the economy as feeding upon the army, becoming nourished by it,
and society's eagerness therefore to support the ratio of
more dead on the battlefield to increased output in production. Brecht's interpretation is not literal, however, as it had
been in *St. Joan*. Rather, in a more Aeschylean style, he
draws upon history and myth to express the contemporary
lesson.

Mother Courage, who has provided each of her three
children with a different father, makes her living as a
tradeswoman by following the Swedish and Imperial
armies during the Thirty Years War. She is a woman who
endures despite the circumstances of war and grows dependent on, and almost fond of, those circumstances. She
does what she has to do to get by. But she does not get by as
far as the fate of her children is concerned. Her sensitive
young daughter, Kattrin, is dumb and mentally retarded—
the effects of a soldier's attack when she was a child. The
eldest son, Eilif, becomes a hero and then is subsequently
executed for the same act performed in different contexts
of war—looting. And the youngest son, Swiss Cheese, an
honest and tender fellow, is executed because he will not
betray his army for the invading one. Mother Courage
could have saved him had she sold her wagon and goods,
but she bargained too long. Kattrin's death is even more
moving, because of all the many persons who pass through
the play, Kattrin alone acts in some small and desperate
way against the war in its most hideous aspects—the slaughter of innocent women and children. Overhearing soldiers
who plot to attack a nearby town, Kattrin beats a drum to
rouse the people in time, but she is discovered and shot by
the men.

These tormenting events overtake Mother Courage's
children not because she intends to expose her children to

harm, but because she thinks she is playing it safe. Eric Bentley expresses this well: "The main reason it doesn't work is that the little world which Mother Courage's wisdom tries to regulate is dependent upon the big world which she has given up as a bad job. Small business is part of the big war which is part of the big business of ownership of *all* the means of production and distribution."[9] Mother Courage simply believes, contrary to tragic theatre, that men and societies have no responsibilities or powers in relation to war; like an inevitable cyclone, it must whip through small people's lives. One should nevertheless learn to make it profitable in the short run of one's own life, as there is nothing that can be done to end it. In the last scene, Mother Courage pays a peasant woman to bury Kattrin, and says as she leaves pulling her indestructible wagon, "I must get back into business."

Although Brecht intended *Mother Courage* to arouse heavily critical feelings on the part of his audiences, most spectators tended to sympathize with Courage's determination to "face" things despite the "sacrifices." This reaction is the sort Brecht had most wanted to expose as wrong, for he believed that the experience of totalitarian regimes during the Second World War would similarly obfuscate their fundamental origins and meaning. In an interview in 1952, he said in relation to this: "The play in question shows that Courage has learnt nothing from the disasters that befall her. The play was written in 1938, when the writer foresaw a great war, he was not convinced that humanity was necessarily going to learn anything from the tragedy which he expected to strike it. . . . But even if Courage learns nothing else at least the audience can, in my view, learn something by observing her."[10]

9. Bentley, tr., *Mother Courage*, Introduction, p. 13.

10. Willett, ed., *Brecht on Theater*, p. 229. Brecht rewrote *Mother Courage* many times, hardening the mother's part in order to encourage the kind of audience response he felt the characterization deserved. Later on Brecht began writing a

Although the mother figure is central to at least four of
Brecht's major plays (for example, the tenacious and
deeply loving Grusha of *The Caucasian Chalk Circle*, who is
the antithesis of Mother Courage), Courage is neither
maternal, especially in the sense of protectiveness and sustenance of progeny, nor courageous. Brecht invokes the
symbolic figure of the mother, rather, in order to establish a
society's predominant character. *Mother Courage* symbolizes
the society that attends to consumption and material security above and beyond its own children's well-being. But the
invocation of the mother figure is intentionally a positive
one: it reveals that society is meant to generate the flow of
life in a liberating sense. Society is intended as Rousseau
and Marx conceived of it, to make men feel as free as they
were in nature without feeling as lonely.

Thus, Brecht's portrayal of Mother Courage should
teach us something about the de-naturing of contemporary
society through war and the affluence that seemed to be its
legacy. Marx and Engels wrote in the *Communist Manifesto*
that "the bourgeois claptrap about the family and education, about the hallowed co-relation of parent and child,
becomes all the more disgusting, the more, by the action of
modern industry, all family ties among the proletarians are
torn asunder and their children transformed into simple
articles of commerce and instruments of labor."[11] Brecht
comes to feel by the time he has written *Galileo* not only that
familial responsibilities have been transformed into instruments of war and commerce, but that society's very purposes are no longer comprehensible to the highly priva-
tized masses of Europe and America. The huge nation-
state, whether democratic or otherwise, had indeed

---

play in answer to Beckett's *Waiting for Godot*, as he observed the "theater of the
absurd" compelling audiences into another sort of indolence, making his own job
that much harder. Brecht died, however, before he finished the counterplay. See
Martin Esslin, *Brecht: The Man and His Work*, p. 102.

11. In Feuer, ed., *Marx and Engels*, p. 25.

become a Leviathan, the provider of wants and the creator of fear. Of the latter, Brecht wrote between 1947 and 1948: "During these wars the mothers of every nation, with their children pressed to them, scan the skies in horror for the deadly inventions of science."[12]

12. Willett, ed., *Brecht on Theater,* pp. 184-185.

11. Workable Pictures of the World

Settling on the fringe of Hollywood in 1941,[1] Brecht continued a strange American sojourn that would culminate in an appearance before the House Committee on Un-American Activities. Now in his mid-forties, he continued writing tragic dramas including his masterpiece, *The Caucasian Chalk Circle*. However, he could find no one in America to publish his poetry, and his coproduction of *Galileo* with Charles Laughton met with an inauspicious response. *Variety's* review stated that "the 'script' did not seem to make the grade and left an overall impression of dullness."[2]

Galileo contains no narrative of an obscure historical era; its dramatization in Beverly Hills in 1947 follows the dropping of the atomic bomb on Hiroshima. It treats directly the issue of the scientist's political responsibility and the impact of scientific and technological advances upon the quality and directions of human life. The fact that American audiences were untouched by the significance of *Galileo* and unmoved by its obvious relevance to their national policies (whereas the anti-Nazi actors of Zurich had achieved great success with it)[3] indicates an erosion of the capacity for critical opinion in its public which is crucial for the sustenance of theatre, and of democracy itself. Within nine years, C. Wright Mills would write in *The Power Elite*: "The most important feature of the public of opinion . . . is the

1. Martin Esslin, *Brecht: The Man and His Work*, p. 72.
2. *Ibid.*, pp. 73, 78-79.
3. *Ibid.*, p. 73.

free ebb and flow of discussion. The possibilities of answering back, of organizing autonomous organs of public opinion, of organizing opinion in action are held to be established by democratic institutions. . . . [However] the issues that now shape man's fate are neither raised nor decided by the public at large."[4] The disappointment of Brecht's reception in the United States is that audiences failed to perceive the central importance of his art for a democratic polity that must depend for its own meaning upon the strengths of its public life. Even the American "left" at this time rejected Brecht's attempts to restore the delicate wholeness of audience, polity, and theatre—partly because the traditional "realist" conventions suited them, and partly because the working class in America has never really disassociated itself from the middle-class.[5]

Brecht's *Galileo* speaks to this aspect of democratic states in an era of totalitarian politics. Brecht had warned that the real legacy of fascism can be even more vicious in a country of so-called "civil liberties" if it destroys freedom of speech.[6] His Galileo gives up the "truth" about the revolution of the earth around the sun because he "does not wish to be smoked like a ham." He steals and adapts a model of the telescope in order to make money. He pursues scientific discovery out of personal vanity and motivations of acquisitiveness. At the heart of his scientific commitment to self is a "natural passivity"[7] that often deters the best of Brecht's characters from a necessary perception of political order and change in relation to their particular vocations. Like Mother Courage and Galy Gay, Galileo sees no need to oppose the existing order of things. But because of the

4. C. Wright Mills, *The Power Elite*, pp. 298, 300.

5. For a more detailed account of Brecht's acrimonious experiences in America and the ways in which he was "banned" from the American stage, see Lee Baxandall, "Brecht in America, 1935," pp. 69-87.

6. From his undelivered statement to the House Committee on Un-American Activities, October 30, 1947.

7. In Eric Bentley, tr., *Seven Plays by Bertolt Brecht*, Introduction to *Galileo*, p. 38.

great import of Galileo's discovery, his passive reticence seems the more heinous.

The first problem raised by *Galileo* is the scientist's cowardice in the face of his society's absolute prohibition against the free exchange of ideas. Galileo is aware of his shortcomings; one of the more memorable scenes is a conversation between the Little Monk and himself, in which he expresses the sort of price his silence is exacting from the Monk's family: "My dear man, as a bonus for not meddling with your parents' peace, the authorities are tendering me, on a silver platter, persecution-free, my share of the fat sweated from your parents, who, as you know, were made in God's image. Should I condone this decree, my motives might not be disinterested: easy life, no persecution, and so on" (scene 7). The Pope expresses the idiosyncracies that Galileo has given to a quality we first encounter in Galy Gay: "He cannot say no to an old wine or a new thought" (scene 11). In order to protect both excesses, Galileo is willing to restrain the obligations of his profession to the truth, as well as he knows it, and to society in terms of its education and needs of subsistence.

The second problem raised in *Galileo*, however, takes us back to Aeschylus' *Prometheus*. It looms large toward the end, as it emerges from Galileo's ironic self-condemnation. He finally asks the essential question of vocation:

> For what reason do you labor? I take it that the intent of science is to ease human existence. If you give way to coercion, science can be crippled, and your new machines may simply suggest new drudgeries. Should you, then, in time, discover all there is to be discovered, your progress must become a progress away from the bulk of humanity. The gulf might even grow so wide that the sound of your cheering at some new achievement would be echoed by a universal howl of horror. . . . Any man who does what I have done must not be tolerated in the ranks of science.
>
> (scene 13)

Brecht is committed, as was Aeschylus, to the belief that technology and scientific discovery must benefit men in their earthly existence, in polities and societies at large. Without some correspondence between the applications of science and a decrease in human suffering, progress has *no* meaning. Aeschylus' response had been to recommend new leadership equipped with a theory of the long-range uses of political power. Brecht, however, is confronted with a far more complicated political and scientific world. There is first for him, as there had not been for the Greeks, the aforementioned schism between state and society, within which small administrative commissions and huge corporations may exercise enormous power over populations they never see and consider only as statistics. Whatever the state's constitution in the twentieth century, self-professed pluralism or elitism, the state will be ruled by bureaucratic institutions or is heading in that direction for survival's sake. Thus, in order to treat the question of a Promethean liberation, Brecht's criticism and appeal must go to the very roots of his political order and to its class conflicts rather than to the Aeschylean precepts of leadership, which presuppose a supportive political environment.

Brecht wants to show that fascism has merely confirmed that the nation-state has not made men free. Commencing with the two cities of Augustine, culminating in Hobbes' political theory, and having undergone industrial and technological revolutions, the contemporary nation has acquired an unprecedented monopoly of economic and political power. Liberty, especially the more fragile kinds— thought and expression in public art—is not cherished within such a political setting. Thus Brecht's theatre portrays the contemporary nation as a polity that must be transformed: what the new forms might be he does not suggest, concentrating instead on the immediate task of reawakening critical minds to the problem. Brecht laments "man's failure to understand the laws governing his life in society. His knowledge of these had not kept pace with his scientific knowledge." Where science has failed, art ought to be able to give, Brecht writes, "a workable picture of the world."[8]

In his last plays, especially the two we are about to discuss, Brecht tries to construct such a workable picture. Throughout, he remains firmly convinced that a dehumanized society can only be salvaged through radical environmental change. In *Galileo,* Brecht had charged the scientific community with having failed in its primary objectives: far from making the world more humanly accessible, it has made us more superstitiously afraid; far from rendering the planet habitable for most, it has only enhanced the comforts of a few. These failings are more than evident to the poorer nations that are often not eager to gain a growing industrial capacity at the cost of an alienated population, new and rising crime rates, and deadly environmental pollution. But to Brecht, the "developed" nations do not as readily perceive that they may be regressing instead of progressing, and they have a low tolerance for this sort of critical evaluation. In order to explore the limitations of social change and the resistance to change as a basic component of all contemporary political life, Brecht turns to the dramatic compositions of China.

Zurich audiences in 1943 saw the first performance of *The Good Woman of Setzuan,*[9] which begins as three Gods have descended to earth in search of a good human being

8. Willett, ed., *Brecht on Theater,* p. 133. What Brecht means at least in part by a "workable picture of the world" is something like what Karl Mannheim implies by the difference between "functional rationalization" and "substantial rationality" in bureaucracies (*Man and Society in an Age of Reconstruction*). Because the worker is confined to one tiny fragment of an entire work process, his own capacity for intelligence and rational insight diminishes. Brecht feels the same thing has happened to all people in modern life, and that the theatre must enable them to see society totally in terms of its interrelations; that theatre is peculiarly equipped to present pictures of the world that "work"—that is, which involve us as thinking persons who can once again meaningfully act and entertain both mystery and simplicity in a common life.

9. Esslin, *Brecht,* p. 313.

willing to offer them a night's lodging. The only person
they can find is Shen Te, a prostitute who must sacrifice a
customer in order to assist them. In reward for her virtue,
they give her enough money to open a small tobacco shop.
People quickly hear of Shen Te's good fortune and pour
into her simple dwelling to take advantage of her known
generosity. She would have been divested of everything
had it not been for her shrewd and unscrupulous cousin,
Shui Ta; he restores order to the shop, settles her debts,
and throws out the parasites. Shen Te later saves a young
man from suicide; hoping for his love, she incurs only more
abuse. When eventually he leaves, she is pregnant and must
provide somehow for herself and the child.

The Gods return to see how Shen Te is faring and find
her cousin, Shui Ta, managing the shop (which has been
expanded into a factory through the ruthless efforts of
himself and Shen Te's lover). Shui Ta claims that he has
not seen Shen Te for months, but Yang Sun, the lover, who
has just returned, claims that he had that very day heard
the sounds of Shen Te crying in the back room of the shop.
The Gods become suspicious and convene a trial to uncover
the whereabouts of Shen Te. During the course of the trial,
Shui Ta suddenly takes off his mask, revealing that he has
been Shen Te all along. She then responds to the Gods:

> . . . yes. Shui Ta *and* Shen Te. Both.
> Your injunction
> To be good and yet to live
> Was a thunderbolt:
> It has torn me in two . . .
> When we extend our hand to a beggar, he tears it
>   off for us
> When we help the lost, we are lost ourselves . . .
> Find me guilty, then, illustrious ones . . .
> For your great, godly deeds, I was too poor, too small.
>   (scene 10)

The Gods prefer to be distracted and rejoice at finding
Shen Te again, refusing to accept what she has had to
become in order to respect their demands. We may be

greatly impressed by how far removed this drama is from
that of Shakespeare's *Lear*, for example, if we try to imagine
Edmund taking off a mask at the end to reveal that he is
also Cordelia, and has had to be Edmund to preserve the
goodness we associate only with Cordelia. This is of course
inconceivable, for Shakespeare assumed that Edmund and
Cordelia belong to two mutually exclusive worlds. He preferred to let Cordelia die untouched by the other world,
rather than expose her to its mutations.

Brecht is in part agreeing with Shakespeare that human
goodness is a total quality that must encompass the political
and social worlds of the person as well as the person
himself. But Brecht has depicted Shen Te as two persons,
one generous and loving and the other equally selfish and
vicious, in order to support the only conclusion he feels is
adequate for contemporary life that would retain some
goodness. The fact is that one learns to be as proficient in
one character as in the other, and it is not so much true for
Brecht that we are all both good *and* bad as that our environments tend to sour whatever natural virtue we might
possess. The Gods sing as they depart:

> What rapture, oh, it is to know
> A good thing when you see it
> And having seen a good thing, oh,
> What rapture 'tis to flee it.

They are happy, like Aeschylus' Oceanos in *Prometheus*, to
flee a painful sight and keep their illusions intact. But
Brecht's conclusion is unmistakable in the Epilogue, which
protests: "a world where the good cannot live surely ought
to be changed"[10] Shen Te cannot avoid playing the role of
her ruthless cousin by becoming a better person, but only
by altering the environment so that she need not be a worse
one.

Between 1944 and 1945, before Brecht returned to East

---

10. The Grove Press translation omits this Epilogue, but Esslin refers to it in *op.
cit.*, p. 314.

Berlin, he finished *The Caucasian Chalk Circle*, which he adapted from an anonymous Chinese play of 1300 A.D., *The Circle of Chalk*, which bears a likeness to the Biblical story of Solomon.[11] The Prologue takes us to Soviet Georgia near the end of World War II, where the members of two collective farms are debating the uses of a certain piece of land. It is finally decided to let the fruit-and-wine collective have the land, because it will prove more productive for all concerned. Afterwards, a folktale is told to reveal the meaning of this decision as it symbolizes the fundamental values of their political life.

The tale begins in feudal Georgia. One day the Governor is slain by rebellious barons, and his wife escapes in terror abandoning her infant son. Grusha, the kitchen maid, rescues the child and takes him on foot upon a treacherous journey to her brother's home in the mountains, where she hopes to be received with sympathy and shelter. At first Grusha wanted to give the child to peasant parents because he would not have the proper parentage with her, and she hesitated to assume her obligation toward him. But at the first sign of real danger from the Ironshirts guards, Grusha retrieves the child, telling him, "Since no one else will take you, son, I must take you now" (scene 2). As in *Mother Courage,* Brecht employs the mother and child relationship in a symbolic enactment of the nature of society and its need for change. The society of the future—the child—can be worthy and compassionate despite its ancestry if it is given the opportunity for productive work. Grusha knows that if she protects the child whom no one wants, his nature will be altered accordingly: thus, Grusha symbolizes contemporary society's assuming this Brechtian "gesture" or attitude toward its own future.

Grusha crosses the glacier and slopes of the northern mountains, and thinks only of how her brother "will rise and embrace" her, how he will say, "I have been expecting

11. Esslin, *Brecht*, p. 318.

you so long" (scene 3). She arrives at last at her brother's lovely house, feeble and ill from the journey. Her brother and his wife rise from their supper, and with an air of embarrassment and annoyance begin to question Grusha, who is not even offered a chair, where she has come from, if the child is hers, if it has a father, where he is, and so on. Grusha begins to cough with cold and faints. The sister-in-law cringes: "If it's consumption we'll all get it." She goes on cross-examining her: "Has your husband got a farm?" When the brother has a few moments alone with Grusha, he adds in mock reassurance: "But you can't stay here long with the child. She's religious, you see" (scene 3).

Through a series of reversals by the end of Part II, the Governor's wife tries to reclaim her lost child, and Grusha must prove, within the familiar Brechtian context of a trial, that she is the "true mother" in order to keep the child she had long labored to protect. Brecht wrote, in his notes on this play, that motherhood may be more socially than biologically determined today. The Judge, Azdak, understands this and like Solomon looks for the ways in which the mother's interests are synonymous with the child's, to determine not who is the mother that gave birth but the mother who would liberate the child.[12] The Judge decides to administer the "famous test of the Chalk Circle" (Part II, scene 2) by drawing a circle of chalk on the floor and placing the boy within it. The Governor's wife, who has been casting asides about the "odour" of the common people, sees Grusha and declares, "Is that the creature?" Grusha, making no claim of blood relationship between the child and herself, states only that she "brought the child up to be friendly with everyone, and from the beginning taught him to work as well as he could."

The child smiles at Grusha from the center of the circle, and as the Judge announces that "the true mother is she

12. Brecht, "On The Caucasian Chalk Circle," pp. 88-100.

who can pull the child out of the circle toward herself," the Governor's wife seizes the child and pulls him out of the circle. Grusha stands by aghast. The Judge performs the test once again to be certain, and Grusha cries in despair, "I brought him up! Shall I tear him to pieces? I can't do it!" The Judge rises, nodding toward Grusha: "And in this manner the Court has established the true mother. Take your child and be off." To the Governor's wife, he declares, "And you disappear before I fine you for fraud" (scene 2).

Brecht's interpretation of this parable reiterates the Aeschylean insight that the real value of political order is not that men are born and bred within it, but that they can become liberated within it through creative work and thought. Therefore, industrial societies must become vehicles of regeneration instead of accumulation; and the child, the future historical society, must be the fruit of commitment to political and social order as a collectivity, instead of to the primacy of competitive self-interest. From the perspective of international conservationists, this is already a truism. From Brecht's focus in this play, to lose possession of progeny is preferable to the child's being torn to pieces. It was Brecht's premonition, however, that European and American societies would surrender to a fatal divisiveness before submitting to the obvious need for change. In both plays we have just discussed, the question of change is as ill-resolved as it is in contemporary politics; but *The Caucasian Chalk Circle's* assertion of the primacy of community over self-interest makes clear the only ways in which political change can effect happy endings. Society and man can be creative of "human" and liberating relationships, Marx wrote in his 1844 "Manuscripts," only if we "assume *man* to be *man*, and his relation to the world to be a human one. Then love can only be exchanged for love, trust for trust, etc. If you wish to enjoy art you must be an artistically cultivated person; . . . Everyone of your relations to man and to nature must be a *specific expression*, corresponding to the object of your will, of your real *individual* life. If you love without evoking love in return . . . then your love is impotent and a misfortune."[13]

By the time he returned to East Berlin in 1947, Brecht had observed various twentieth-century political cultures and continued to believe that theatre must reveal European and American societies' inability to achieve, for all their scientific and technological achievements, human and liberating environments. The scientific and democratic state was, for Brecht, still a state of the future. From 1949 until his death in 1956, Brecht did enjoy, however, for the first time the relaxed artistic freedom of his own theatre group, the Berliner Ensemble, in his East Berlin Theatre am Schiffbauerdamm. Although his existence in communist Europe was sometimes difficult, he appreciated the opportunities for experimentation and the enthusiasm of educated audiences, which he had rarely encountered elsewhere in the world.[14] His Theatre am Schiffbauerdamm seats 700 persons; it bears no resemblance to the open-air Theatre of Dionysos or to the three-tiered Globe of Shakespear's London. It is equipped with film and recording effects, has a mobile stage with several levels, but its function and purpose was for Brecht the same as that of all previous theatre: to educate its spectators to a critical vision of all collective life. To this end, he had developed over his creative years a theory of the Epic Theatre, and more specifically began to adapt certain works from the classics to the new needs of the German theatre in the 1950s. An unpublished note of Brecht's refers to the "historic line of the Epic Theatre as running from the Elizabethan drama via Lenz, Schiller (early works), Goethe (*Götz* and both parts of *Faust*), Grabbe, Büchner."[15] Making these historical connections

13. Bottomore, tr., *Karl Marx, Early Writings*, pp. 193-194.
14. See Esslin's Part III, "The Pitfalls of Commitment," in *Brecht: The Man and His Work.*
15. R. Manheim and J. Willett, trs., *Bertolt Brecht, Collected Plays*, Vol. 9, Introduction, p. xiii.

through adaptations was an integral part of his Epic Theatre conception of drama, for Brecht wanted both dramatist and audience to be capable of productively using the past in the present. He viewed the theatre materials of other times as *living* in a far-reaching present but requiring certain idiosyncratic modifications to be restaged in the present. An excellent case in point is his *Coriolanus*, adapted of course from Shakespeare.

Brecht's version follows the original closely with the significant exception of Brecht's Act Five, Scene 4. In this scene, Coriolanus is visited by his mother, wife, and son, who plead for a merciful retreat by the Volscian troops then marching upon Rome. In Shakespeare's play, the mother-son confrontation is the decisive moment of the drama. Coriolanus is passionately swayed and ultimately destroyed by his mother's appeal to family loyalty and the attending feelings of patria this loyalty must command. Thus, Shakespeare's Tullus Aufidius declaims Coriolanus' seeming surrender to his mother's guilt-inducing invectives in these words: "I am glad thou hast set thy mercy and thy honour At difference in thee: out of that I'll work myself a former fortune" (V. iii. 203-5). To Shakespeare, even this power-driven Coriolanus can be tempered by mercy and maternal cries. For Brecht this scene is important for precisely the opposite lesson. Brecht deemphasizes this scene to reinforce the conclusion that in *Coriolanus*, power very nearly overrides every competing loyalty. Obsessive in its self-centeredness, political power dotes on its own specific objectives, and Coriolanus is simply its immediate pawn. In the end, as Brecht puts it, the *context* of political power determines the fates of various political actors: "The storm puts out the fire it has fanned. Nail drives out nail and power by power's unmanned" (Act Four, Scene 4).

From this adaptation and between the two playwrights' interpretations of political power, we can see a world that has continually hardened, that is even less amenable to

human feeling in relation to power than it was in Shakespeare's time. Brecht's political world has shattered the
competitors; power is worshipped for its indiscriminate
appetites—it flaunts international aspirations, it knows no
boundaries technological or human, and it is what moves
the world, what must move Coriolanus for him to remain
real for us. There must be less logic in his destruction,
except for the logic of men in power: they are merely
consumed. Coriolanus' decision to march or not to march
on Rome is not what matters most to Brecht. It is the power
situation of blinding city rivalries and family pride in which
he operates that must be changed, or no decision will lead
to a constructive political outcome for Coriolanus or his
people.

Coriolanus was the product of Brecht's later years, but
when he first began to think about his Epic theatre, his
worst obstacle was not theatre's unpopularity (which considering the drama's banality was rather a hopeful sign) but
the long-standing traditions of theatre as illusion. Brecht
formulated his principles of theatre in contradiction to two
classical German criteria for drama, criteria derived from
Aristotle's *Poetics* and Goethe's and Schiller's dramatic
works. While he agreed with Aristotle's emphasis on the
centrality of narrative in drama, he denied completely, as
Aeschylus would have, the purpose of sheer catharsis
without a theory of political education. Empathy is unpro-
ductive if it does not "correspond to the sociological situation."[16] Brecht writes in his *Short Organum for the Theater*
(1947-1948), "what . . . Aristotle demanded of tragedy is
nothing higher or lower than that it should entertain
people. Theater may be said to be derived from ritual, but
that is only to say that it becomes theater once the two have
separated; what it brought over from the mysteries was not
its former ritual function, but purely and simply the
pleasure which accompanied this."[17]

16. Willett, ed., *Brecht on Theater*, p. 21.
17. *Ibid.*, p. 181.

Whatever else Brecht demanded of theatre, he believed that the experience of pleasure, as Shakespeare had evoked it and as it characterizes Oriental theatres, is the most authentic experience in drama. Of course, not just any form of entertainment is pleasurable. Brecht estimated that the level of public pleasure fluctuates according to the accuracy of the theatre's reconstructions of life.

It is the inaccurate way in which happenings between human beings are represented that restricts our pleasure in the theater. The reason: we and our forebears have a different relationship to what is being shown. . . . That is to say, our representations must take second place to what is represented, men's life together in society; and the pleasure felt in their perfection must be converted into the higher pleasure felt when the rules emerging from this life in society are treated as imperfect and provisional. In this way the theater leaves its spectators productively disposed even after the spectacle is over.[18]

His harshest critique on the subject of inaccuracy in theatre was reserved for romanticism and the theatre of the absurd, which he argued devote major creative energies to explorations of consciousness completely excluding political and social realities. Brecht felt this "theater of destiny" leaves the more taxing and less penetrable dilemmas of human existence unaddressed. As Werner Mittenzwei suggested during a Symposium in 1968, Brecht regarded the representation of a man who does not know who he is, who is alienated by definition or in essence, as an abstraction not even of man but of ineluctable fate. As such, Mittenzwei continues, this representation is contrary to the essential function of theatre, which is to transform the world. It will not do this directly, in the crude, idealist sense. Rather, by "rendering visible the invisible processes of society, by bringing to consciousness that which is unconscious, the theater becomes a social force and can contribute to real change."[19] In addition, theatre does not regard as authentic

18. *Ibid.*, pp. 183, 205.
19. Freely translated and paraphrased from the French translation of the German, "Mouvement Perpetuel ou Fin de Partie (Brecht sur les scenes du

a choice *between* political and psychological themes. Once again, it by nature addresses itself to the broadest regions of human life.

Brecht's development of these points in theatre became his own "realist" perspective, which in the 1930s began to challenge that of George Lukacs.[20] He intended his Epic theatre to improve upon realism through various measures. By preventing the spectator from becoming involved in a seductive and stupefying plot, the Epic theatre would compel him instead to recognize his own capacity for action, to stand outside the play's experience and take the human being as an object of inquiry rather than as a fixed point for arousing pity or fear.[21] For the Epic theatre to accomplish this task, it had also to pull the audience away from illusion and transport it back into judgment, action, and construction. This is one of the reasons many major plays by Brecht transform the audience into juries by incorporating a trial scene.

Alienation, far from being the essential human condition, is the first measure of instruction in Brecht's Epic theatre. As he wrote, "When something seems 'the most obvious thing in the world' it means that any attempt to understand the world has been given up."[22] Brecht borrowed alienation effects from Chinese acting in which actors wear masks, paint their faces, and employ symbols in an effort to hinder simple identification with characters in a play. Basically, these effects help the actor project his awareness of being seen by the spectators and as a result make everything else appear strange and amazing. The actor's self-awareness and contact with the audience disintegrates the "fourth wall." The audience can no longer

---

monde)," by Werner Mittenzwei, in *Recherches Internationales*, No. 60 (1969); Mittenzwei is the author of *Bertolt Brecht; Von der 'Massnahme' zum 'Leben des Galilei'* (Aufbau Verlag, East Berlin, 1962).

20. Willett, ed., *Brecht on Theater*, p. 109.
21. *Ibid.*, p. 37.
22. *Ibid.*, p. 71.

preserve an illusion of standing outside the performance in invisible seclusion. When the actor self-consciously regards his own action with surprise, he catches the audience unaware, and lifts mundane things "above the level of the obvious and automatic."[23] The audience must suddenly see the drama's world as its own and can no longer ignore theatre by comparing it disadvantageously to "real life." On the contrary, the pictures evoked upon the stage are to be transported, through the audience's recollection, out of the theatre into the world, where they more obviously fit.

The specific uniqueness of the Epic theatre is its restoration of two Aeschylean principles of drama: that theatre originates in the foundations of political and social life, for which it becomes a crossroads; and that theatre's most pressing objective is the political education of the spectator. Althusser speaks of the second principle in his essay on materialist theatre:

To produce a new, true and active consciousness in his spectators, Brecht's world must necessarily exclude any pretensions to exhaustive self-recovery and self-representation in the form of a consciousness of self. . . . That is why . . . for him (I am still discussing the "great plays") no character consciously contains in himself the totality of the tragedy's conditions. . . . In these plays the centre is always to one side, if I may put it that way . . . the centre is always deferred, always in the beyond, in the movement going beyond illusion towards the real.[24]

Brecht's Epic theatre, although influential and fashionable today, has had much less impact upon Europe and America than Aeschylean theatre had upon the Mediterranean world, even in terms of rejection. When the Athenians under Pericles had had enough of Aeschylean political criticism and inquiry, they went on to witness less political but nevertheless profound drama. Aeschylean tragedy had at the very least established extraordinary criteria for tragic

23. *Ibid.*, p. 92.
24. Louis Althusser, tr., *For Marx*, pp. 143, 144, 145.

drama which extended beyond Aeschylus' own period of
theatre. But Brecht did not find ready acceptance during
his own creative period, and has not yet established a tradition—except among select groups of the intelligentsia
scattered throughout the world (Lyubimov in the Soviet
Union, Utpal Dutt in Bengal, the Living Theatre in New
York, for example).

One of the questions confronting the student of Brecht,
within the scope of this study, is why his theatre has not
been established as a great public theatre in the traditions
of Aeschylus and Shakespeare.[25] A. C. Bradley suggested
in 1923 one possible answer, "that Greek tragedy represents the total Greek mind more fully than modern tragedy
can the total modern mind."[26] Brecht himself anticipated
this problem of theatre in the twentieth century when he
asked if the present-day world could be reproduced by
means of theatre. His answer, written shortly before his
death in 1955, contains the following ideas:

For it is because we are kept in the dark about the nature of
human society—as opposed to nature in general—that we are
now faced . . . by the complete destructibility of this planet that
has barely been made fit to live in. . . . You may perhaps agree
with me that the present-day world can do with transforming. . . .
It may be enough if I anyway report my opinion that the present-
day world can be reproduced even in the theater, but only if it is
understood as being capable of transformation.[27]

One may certainly wonder if Brecht's theatre has had less
impact upon contemporary societies not because of any

25. Lee Baxandall writes: "And while Brecht now is rather often produced
commercially in New York and the regional theatres, this 'success' seems to stem
less from an understanding of the genuine Brecht than from the world stature of
the man and a willingness to misrepresent his theatre practice in whole or in
part. . . . Paul Peters [suggested] the case against an American Epic Theatre break-
through: 'For the time being (then and now) Brecht may be too sophisticated, too
new, too special for most theatre-goers and for workers.' " In "Brecht in America,
1935," pp. 86-87.
26. *Oxford Lectures on Poetry*, p. 95.
27. Willett, ed., *Brecht on Theater*, p. 275.

inherent problem in his uses of the art form but because these societies have resisted his focus upon social transformation. Brecht's theatre has not shunned its vocational obligations to the contemporary mind, however fragmented it may be; it is rather that industrial societies of the twentieth century cannot, or will no longer, collectively witness critical visions of themselves upon a stage in which social action is dramatized as necessary and even constructive. But to discuss this question more adequately, we must move on to the larger issue of theatre's potential meanings in our present world societies.

12. The Political Vocation of Theatre

Even the bursting flood of a vast catastrophe can be
appreciated in all its majesty by society, if society knows
how to master it; then we make it our own. . . . Let us
hope that their theatre may allow them to enjoy as entertainment that terrible and never-ending labour which
should ensure their maintenance together with the terror
of their unceasing transformation.

Brecht, *A Short Organum for the Theater*

Since Brecht's death, many able critics of drama have
expressed an impatience with the conundrum that seems to
incarnate his life and work. What are we to do, they ask,
with a dramatist who is constantly changing, moving from
crude ideology in the 1920s to a working self-criticism and
expansive sensitivity in his later years; a dramatist whose
theories of drama are far better known than his own plays
and yet whose "idea of a theatre" remains just as homeless
as the existing European and American theatres are eclec-
tic, fragmented, and without focus?[1] What are we to do with
a man who burst through the fourth wall only to spend his
life behind others, whose world significance far outweighs
his actual theatre activity, and whose real audience seems
only now to be gathering? Most of all, what are we to do
with Brecht's tiresome tragic optimism—his interpretation
of Hitler's rise to power as the "resistible ascent" of a
Chicago gangster, his workable pictures of the world, his
urgings that we make catastrophes our own, find pleasure

1. Francis Ferguson has suggested that today's unrealized idea of a theatre
reveals society's unrealized center, its unaffirmed self, its isolation and lack of
collective focus, in *The Idea of a Theater*, p. 239.

in jarring transformations of our values, and even experience demons joyfully (a demand more comprehensible to
Asian audiences than to rationalized Westerners, who
prefer demons on the proper terrain). It is Brecht's virtue
of being in-between that invites the frustration. His theatre
stands between East and West, borrowing from both and
addressing both as one; it dramatized the current world
situation, but for audiences that did not exist in the
present; it reimposed an Aeschylean sense of action upon a
theatre universe dominated largely by action occurring in
unrelated and absurd episodes;[2] it deplored the hypocrises
of religion while pressing the need for human salvation; it
was frankly socialist in outlook and professional commitment, but mercilessly self-corrective.[3] If only Brechtian
theatre had been less tolerant of divisions (which from this
study's perspective would make it less of a theatre), it might
have produced a Theatre of the Absurd at its best, and like
Beckett's *Endgame*, taught us something painfully harder to
extract about new beginnings and transformations. But
then Brecht would have had to forsake for a rare great play
an overall idea of theatre. And he would have had to ignore
what he knew too well: that attempted new beginnings had
actual meaning in the world mainly outside of Europe and
America; and that theatre at the very least had to keep in
touch with these world events while remaining sensitive to
the philosophical disenchantments of Western culture.

Or Brecht might have shown more singleminded devotion to the Asian theatre from which he drew so much
inspiration by establishing with Artaud a Theatre of Cruelty that would deny the very substance of any "Western"

2. Brecht wrote, "Every act comes from a realization. There's really no such
thing as acting on impulse . . . the intellect is lurking in the background." Willett,
ed., *Brecht on Theater*, p. 16.

3. Manfred Wekwerth informs us that toward the end of his life, Brecht
avoided even his notion of Epic theatre. It was for him only a conception that
paved the way for theatres still to be constructed. He indulged in none of the
rigidities and pretensions of ideological cant. In Wekwerth, "From Brecht
Today," tr. Martin Nicolaus, pp. 123-124.

dramatic form. But there again, Brecht would have lost his idea of theatre by obliterating the social, historical, and political contexts within which each theatre must live; his choice of an Asian mysticism might have seemed as foreign to its Balinese counterpart as to his European observers. A theatre designed to save the dramatist from his own world simply places the disease in the art form itself. For Brecht, spectators had to treat the theatre as they would a laboratory, a place to observe experiments in action which are related to the afflicted world they must re-enter after the theatre play. Audiences were to feel their intelligence and judgment intimately involved in the outcome of these experiments, as if they had to do with cancer research; they were to feel no emotional identification, and certainly not the distractions of trance. As Jan Kott has mentioned, Artaud himself realized how far he had strayed, in his own terms, from an art of drama when in 1927 he wrote: "It is certain that if I had created a theatre, what I would have done would have had as little relation to that which we are in the habit of calling 'theatre,' as the representation of some obscenity resembles an ancient religious mystery."[4]

Or Brecht might have placed all his artistic energy at the disposal of his Epic theatre conception alone, and become embroiled in the 1960s Theatre of Happenings debate over theatre as stageless, textless environment versus theatre as an interpretive instrument for stage and script. Once again, he would have given us no idea of a theatre to underlie diverse plays, and the living socio-political context that is so much a part even of his Epic theatre would have been swallowed up in the fury over theatre formality, nudity, and stage conventions. It is not that these various theatre interpretations have had nothing to offer, or even have offered too little, but that in all their creative diversity they give little or no attention to the *reasons* for the atrophy of

4. Quoted in Jan Kott, "Witkiewicz and the Corpses; On the Dialectic of Anachronism," p. 66.

European and American dramatic arts, the very reasons that spark their search for new forms. These reasons can only be found in the essential relationships which theatre shares with its polity and society. Brecht not only managed to confront these relationships (though at the cost of sometimes tedious breadth), but was almost alone in his understanding that, as Fergusson had warned us, twentieth-century audiences are presented with a plethora of plays but no idea of a theatre that can address the complexities and contradictions of the age. Even though the complexities may be more intense than in any previous historical era, Brecht took upon himself the task of constructing such a theatre, knowing that this task, as Fergusson did not tell us, is irreducibly political in its parts and horizons.

An idea of a theatre is political first because of what the theatre has always meant and must always be: a place of collective memory and for seeing. That *seeing* has always been experienced in relationships of the polity: those who see (the audience), those who enact the vision (the actors), and that which is seen are parts of the same collective life. That collective life had once been a vision of the city, at other times of the state and the nation, and in each historical instance the living theatre has also envisioned, in Brecht's words, some workable picture of the world. Of course, the "world" has been known to extend variously from Gibraltar to the Red Sea, or from Peking to the Great Wall, or from London to New Delhi and so on. But today, Brecht has tried to tell us, those many former worlds, measured against the barbarian peripheries from which their cultures were shielded, can no longer work for us. Dramatic art, and certainly science, must address themselves now to an entire planet which is technologically unified. They must betray no enthnocentricities, and theatre cannot, except at its peril, disinherit its larger audiences of the future.

Thus, ironically, when European and American theatre arts are less disposed to contemplating a theatre that is

defined as political in audience and vision, Brecht insisted
that theatre today is more political than it has ever been
before. This he asserted not because of his own socialist
politics but because the subject matters of theatre must
reflect changing world realities.[5] As C. Wright Mills had
reminded us, in our own time and for better or for worse,
the world has been permanently sliced up into nations. In
our daily lives we have become dependent upon international events that at another historical juncture might
never have touched us. When the whole earth has become a
single network of nations, no one nation's political life and
culture, no matter how seemingly remote, can long remain
immune to the unsettling currents of distant shores. And,
as one might expect from the characteristics of theatre set
forth in this study, it is where the tensions between polity,
traditional religion, the outside world, and social change
are greatest, from an international perspective, that theatre
activity will be most intense. Of this there is more to say
shortly; the point to be made here is that theatre, at the very
least, must live in the largest possible regional context of
language and collective historical experience,[6] and it must
remain open in its presentations to all the world's societies,
upon which it is in some ways dependent and for which, in
quite other ways, it is responsible.

Thus the idea of a theatre is political: first because it must
make possible the enactment of an actual political world in
the midst of painful and complex transformations within

5. Elizabeth Hauptmann, Brecht's collaborator, wrote in her diary in 1926:
[Brecht] "had concluded that the old (great) form of drama wasn't fit for repre-
senting such modern processes as the international distribution of wheat, the life
stories of people of our times and generally for all events with consequences."
Quoted in Darko Suvin, "The Mirror and the Dynamo. On Brecht's Aesthetic
Point of View," p. 63, note 5.

6. A. J. Guanwardana has made this point in relation to our appreciation of
Asian drama: "That a theatre can be fully understood only when firmly located in
its context has yet to be recognized in the field of Asian theatre studies as a whole."
"Theatre in Asia: An Introduction," p. 49.

and between polities; and second, because of its most decisive component, its audience. In considering that audience, however, we find ourselves confronted with the most puzzling aspect of Brecht's theatre reconstructions. Brecht's own life experience as a dramatist afforded incontestible proof that theatre audiences could no longer be synonymous with nations or cities as they had been in the classical eras of Aeschylus and Shakespeare, and that in Europe and America theatre had even become dislodged from the state. How could an audience comprising a mere fragment of its own society, if that, and scattered exiles and emigrés, be political in the same sense as the citizen audiences of Athens and London? The answer was obviously that they could not. But Brecht spent most of his creative life in exile himself, and by the time he had a theatre and city of his own in East Berlin, he knew both that the audience had to be reconstituted and that he had not composed his dramas for contemporaries.

This is what is so strange about Brechtian drama, and what probably repels European and American societies, which have foresaken their futures for an ageless present, and it is probably what attracts Third World societies which often wish to dramatize their future as opposed to a despairing present. Brecht's audience was an audience yet unborn, or just beginning to assume its dimensions in our own time. If it would not be political by citizenship, it would be political in the most ancient sense of political theory: spectators would be engaged once more in the quest for just polities, for collective orders and symbols through which they would begin to relearn and recollect a thwarted humanity. In a Brechtian pun, the audience would retrieve its vocation of minding the state—as both participant and critical interpreter of public life. The ideal spectator would be one who would look for "the unrealized potentialities in each stage of human development, [for] tensions between a humanizing possibility and specific social alienations. . . .

Reality [would be] seen as interacting processes in an experience of painful humanization."[7]

Other European dramatists and directors with less far-sighted audience expectations have not only denied the political vocation of theatre but would deprive it of any vocation whatsoever. In contrast to Brecht, Jerzy Grotowski, for example, was not reluctant to make this confession a few years ago in New York: "I think that the theatre as an art-form is dying. . . . I can't inspire confidence in other people about this since I don't feel any myself." The journalist conducting the interview adds: "He went on to claim that the feverish theatrical activity going on all around us is to be attributed to those who have felt this fundamental doubt and . . . want to stifle it with the sound and fury of new methods."[8] For Mr. Grotowski, as for American theatre in general, the theatre is primarily a business.[9] It would then presumably "die" like any commercial enterprise from lack of consumer response. And in contrast to Brecht's suggestion that the classics be adapted to contemporary needs, Mr. Grotowski's statement implies that historical theatres have no meaning for twentieth-century audiences. The journalist goes on to tell us that for Grotowski, "although theatrical knowledge is many centuries old, it is of no importance. It can be discarded."[10] What it really means, however, to say that theatre as an art form is dying is something Mr. Grotowski has not told us. Because the drama is a society's living art, an art bound up in a political order's meaning and history, it is not possible to "individualize" the theatre out of its sociopolitical context;

7. Darko Suvin, "The Mirror and the Dynamo," p. 60.

8. Quoted in Frank Jotterand, "Theater as an Art-Form is Dying," *Le Monde Weekly*, February 24, 1971, p. 7.

9. See, for example, Jack Poggi, *Theater in America; the Impact of Economic Forces, 1870-1967*; and Robert Gard, *Grassroots Theater, A Search for Regional Arts in America*.

10. Jotterand, "Theatre as an Art-Form is Dying."

and we might wish to resist such a generalization that so poorly represents contemporary world theatres. The existence of theatre as an art form today is, I believe, much more complicated, and many countries have apparently missed Grotowski's death notice because they persist in supporting local, regional, and national theatres that explore Eastern and Western dramatic and political traditions.

One such report on the state of the art in Asia is given us by A. J. Guanwardana, who claims that "Asian theatre, as a whole, is *changing*—some forms are dying, others are renewing themselves, new ones are evolving—as the societies themselves are undergoing transformations at all levels."[11] The ancient forms that are dying, largely in south and southeast Asia, where theatre materials were drawn for centuries from the classical Indian epics *Mahabharata* and *Ramayana*, have lost their audiences in the traumatic experiences of "modern social change," a growing middle-class and proletariat, and forced migrations from rural villages to cities. Local folk cultures have been irreparably altered by colonial rule and its economic and administrative procedures, even in Indonesia, where the Dutch rulers attempted in some respects to protect indigenous art forms.[12] Among the theatre forms that are renewing themselves and evolving, Guanwardana has included a group of "intermediary theatres" that provide some of the more interesting examples of theatre's political vocation. These theatres are intermediary because they are not totally grounded in classical cultures: "they are traditional in form but project secular values."[13] More recent secular influences have been Marxist, emanating mainly from China

11. Guanwardana, "Theatre in Asia: An Introduction," p. 49.
12. *Ibid.*, pp. 52, 54-55.
13. *Ibid.*, p. 55. These theatres include Kabuki, Chinese Opera, the Jatra, Nautanki, and Tamasha of India, the Likay of Thailand, the Malaysia Bangsawan, and the Ludruk of Indonesia. He notes that the "politicizing" of intermediary theatres has been an internal and voluntary process.

and sometimes even from Brecht's Epic theatre. An illustration of this approach to theatre can be found in the dramas of Kateb Yacine, Algeria's fine playwright who emerged in the revolutionary war years of the late 1950s and early 1960s.

In what follows, four distinct interpretations of the political vocation in Asian theatres will be briefly discussed so that the protean nature of theatre's political vocation may be made more comprehensible, and the sense of Brecht's "theatre of instruction" be given more living substance. These four theatres are not meant to represent categories of the art form; and a good deal of theatre activity in Turkey, other parts of the Near East, and in North Africa and South America will be necessarily neglected. But it is hoped that a glance at these four theatres will heighten our expectations of diversity in all contemporary national drama and theatre forms.

At one extreme, Utpal Dutt's Bengali Jatra theatre presents dramas for the purpose of effecting immediate and limited political action. In 1966, a year of dreadful famine in Bengal, Bihar, and Assam, communist leaders were jailed. Using the famine as a central theme in songs and plays, the Jatra theatre group managed to provoke demonstrations throughout Bengal, ultimately securing the government's release of prisoners by March 1967. Jatra is a theatre in the round, of forceful vocal contrasts, whose audience is mainly the working class. It appeals to local populations in urban and rural areas by dramatizing present-day political crises in ways that illuminate the spectators' relationships to the events and their potentials for revolutionary action and change. Dutt credits Brecht and Gorki with providing the most significant dramatic perceptions for his own theatre's needs.[14]

China's opera and ballet combine diverse elements of music, dance, and drama from East and West, and their

14. A. J. Guanwardana, "Theatre as a Weapon," pp. 226-236.

audiences approximate the citizen-audiences of old. Women lend vitality and originality to the epic ballets, such as *The White Haired Girl*. But the repertoire is still quite restricted by the state, and Brecht's characteristic self-correction and criticism do not seem to permeate these theatre productions, though he has had some influence in Peking. What one discovers in China is a ritualizing of the revolution, the founding political act, but in a manner peculiar to Asian traditional drama: emphasis is placed upon the performance and interpretation of a well-known play rather than upon the addition of new compositions, as in Europe and America. The sense of action is, to a limited degree, Aeschylean and Brechtian, in that political change, scientific and technological achievements, and the improvement of the citizens' lives must correspond to each other; but the state appears to be more restrictive with its theatre, and so the ambitions for political action in the future are largely shown as reenactments of recent history.[15] Tensions are dramatized in relation to the pre-Maoist past.

Ludruk drama in Java is a fascinating half-way point between Bengali Jatra theatre, which is still searching out its revolutionary polity, and Chinese opera, which celebrates its existing revolutionary polity. Ludruk is a special interpreter of the polity in transition and recalls the collective memory to its essential tasks by constituting audiences as thoughtful commentators on their own severe displacements from village to city. These audiences, often new tenants from the country or townspeople straining against new facets of urbanization, observe themselves in the process of changing socially and politically. The wide-ranging humor of the stage presentations helps them to live with (as Shakespeare might have said) the modernity for which they are compelled to barter their past. In Indonesia,

15. See Uchiyama Jun, "Doctrine: China, Theatre After 1949," tr. by Tomoko Kusuhara, pp. 252-257.

in general, "drama still transmits sociopolitical ideals between the court (or city) and the countryside and reinforces religious traditions; live theatre is still a vital and popular teacher."[16]

The teachings of this drama have undergone some transitions of their own. Always focusing on the city (portrayed as *madju*, a "progressive" place),[17] Ludruk drama features a clown and a transvestite singer. The clown is a carryover from traditional Wayang shadow-puppet plays who speaks for the "little man" or lower classes; and the transvestite permits women, who are still prohibited from stage performance, to play strong roles in dramatic reenactments. During the Sukarno years, the ideal spectator of Ludruk was proletarian and communist. He was encouraged to adopt urban dress and manners; and as Peacock concluded, Ludruk instilled in its audiences the prescriptions of bureaucratic rationality and the ambitions of upward social mobility.[18] Theatre productions since 1966, however, have turned away from proletarian themes to project a more balanced and often wry assessment of urban life. "Progress" is dramatized now with its two heads, one cool and determined, the other more regretful and ambivalent (reminiscent of Brecht's *Good Woman of Setzuan*). Not all means to social advancement are depicted as acceptable.[19] This remarkable theatre acts as timekeeper for its society, translating regional languages into Javanese, village shyness into city assertiveness, and a not very mechanized local universe into a national political culture. The audiences are not fooled; being up-to-date can be more illusory and less rewarding than advertised. The little people continue to find themselves symbolized by the clown whose pain is enacted as laughter.

16. Barbara Hatley, "Wayang and Ludruk Polarities in Java," pp. 88, 95.
17. *Ibid.*, p. 95.
18. See James L. Peacock, *Rites of Modernization: Symbolic and Social Aspects of Indonesian Proletarian Drama.*
19. Hatley, "Wayang and Ludruk Polarities in Java," pp. 96-98.

Our last example comes from another Indonesian country, Bali, whose theatre is processional and ruler-centered as were the street theatres of fifteenth- and sixteenth-century England. However, Balinese drama is politically meaningful in ways unique to this island. In the plural histories of theatres and their polities, Bali constitutes, as Clifford Geertz has interpreted it for us, a "theatre-state": "Court ceremonialism was the driving force of court politics. Mass ritual was not a device to shore up the state; the state was a device for the enactment of mass ritual. To govern was not so much to choose as to perform. Ceremony was not form but substance. Power served pomp, not pomp power."[20] Bali presents us with a theatre whose vocation is political (actors are kings and princes, the audience peasant-citizens) but also a state whose vocation is dramatic. The polity's essential manifestation rests in its self-portrayal; its action is an acting out of what Geertz has called the people's "place within an eternal metaphysical order that matters"; and its tensions are profoundly religious and political.[21] It is as if the Balinese had undertaken to inhabit Prospero's island after his departure, as if they had endured with him the tempest of his powers, witnessed their inefficacies and learned the terrible lesson of state: that the ceremonies of healing, communion with the divine, and community affection may be its only realities, while pursuits of power are its self-destructive plays of diversion. Balinese drama's quest for political centeredness takes the art of recollection into unfamiliar and imposing territory.

After these brief excursions into Asian drama, it should be more difficult to speak of theatre as an art form that is dying. Just as the needs of its critical vision and the tensions between spiritual and material worlds do not easily die, theatres continue to enable the spectator to see his society in its wholeness, its interrelationships and structures of

20. Clifford Geertz, *The Interpretation of Cultures; Selected Essays*, p. 335.
21. *Ibid.*, p. 390.

power, and thus to seal his action in its living context. The point is that theatre has historically performed an educational function for political life which no other art form or political institution can perform as well. The theatre dies only when its audiences no longer require this education and no longer locate intelligence at the remote outposts of collective memory. Even Grotowski, in a moment of nostalgia, claimed that only the theatre "gives us the opportunity to stop lying."[22] Theatre accomplishes this not because it dramatizes a truth, but because it dramatizes many truths including some that are no longer true. As in Aeschylean tragedy, theatre portrays a polity's on-going present in light of its history and future. It threads events both horizontally through time and vertically across political and social distinctions such as class, region, and faith, so that each spectator is made to relive the political situation of other members of his polity. Theatre constructs this total vision also through an invisible war of words and acts.[23] Where dialogue in isolation may over time acquire a reality contrary to its original meaning, words followed by concentrated action perform a function of defamiliarization, as Brecht would say. We know Richard III far better by his acts than by his words, but it is Shakespeare's play that enables us to know the difference.

In addition to portraying human action on levels of history, polity, and the relationship between words and deeds, theatre is the sole institution that presents a society to itself, apart from its predominant self-image. Newspapers, television, and cinema do not as readily report the

22. Jotterand, "Theatre as an Art-Form is Dying."
23. This subject, mentioned in passing here and given some attention in Part II on Shakespeare, has constituted the center of many analyses in linguistic philosophy and literary criticism and would certainly require a study of its own. I would refer the reader once again to Stanley Cavell's *Must We Mean What We Say? A Book of Essays,* especially his essay on *King Lear,* "The Avoidance of Love," and to selected portions of Susanne Langer's two volumes, *Mind; An Essay on Human Feeling.*

news or provide entertainment from minority perspectives within their own or foreign societies. And the predominant view of a society can usually be presented as merely one view, instead of *the right view*, within the context of a theatre whose audience confronts internal conflicts and contradictions.

Finally, as theatre provides the wider and unfragmented vision of a particular society and culture, it can enable people—especially in large industrial societies—to recover the spirit of action and participation in public life of which excessive concern for individualism and privacy has deprived them.[24] Theatre conveys an underlying unity necessary to any constructive action and accessible to people who are witnesses to a common life. A people that has the courage to witness critically its government and society in action should be capable of believing in itself as a whole and reassuming responsibility for actions on the level of the state. The twentieth-century fascist regimes of Hitler, Mussolini, and Franco were cognizant of the power of great public gatherings and often staged them in stadiums and coliseums. But these fascist states, though they had newspapers and movies, could never have produced a single theatre. Their purpose was not to educate the mass into a thoughtful political body but to stimulate and make use of its blind energies for the purposes of domination. This is why when one speaks of theatre as "political," it makes all the difference in the world whether this means a critical vision of all political life or the ruler's exercise in totalitarian control, which has not been the theatre's forte.

When Brecht appeared before the House Committee on Un-American Activities in 1947, he prepared a statement

24. Martin Esslin refers to this in his chapter "The Role of Theatre" as the "spontaneous human experience" which is "more and more disappearing through the cancerous growth of overorganized, overmechanized . . . patterns of work, behavior, thought . . . . The genuine need for a theatre is growing apace—for a theatre in which human beings can regain their autonomy of feeling." *Reflections: Essays on Modern Theatre*, p. 220.

which he was not permitted to read aloud. In it, he wrote: "Looking back at my experiences as a playwright and a poet in the Europe of the last two decades, I wish to say that the great American people would lose much and risk much if they allowed anybody to restrict free competition of ideas in cultural fields, or to interfere with art, which must be free in order to be art."[25] Restriction of freedom in art can take many forms. In America, it is largely a voluntary submission by the people and professionals of journalism, movies, and television to neglect an essential public obligation, a political obligation that Brecht, more than any other contemporary dramatist, made visible for us. As Walter Benjamin phrased it, there is "a distinction between the operative and the informative writer. The mission of the operative writer is not to report, but to fight, not to be the audience but to play an active part."[26] This is, then, the political vocation of drama: to remind a society of its obligation to act in terms of its constructive well-being, not as a self-interested power among nations but as a large community among other collectivities burdened by equally painful pasts and confronted by equally pessimistic futures. Drama interprets for us the political commitment to act in face of terrible contradictions, to tolerate hopelessness, to work with a limited and defective world, and while accepting its various deaths, to play out our lives with some dignity.

Theatre, seen in this vein, is far too threatening a public art for a society that cannot face itself, its past, or its domestic and international uses of power. A nation that, like Mother Courage, has little motivation to learn anything from its history, or the histories of other societies, is more consistent in not reserving its cerebral and public spaces for the magnificent, brooding, and critical theatres. For theatre's vocation has always been and will always be to present

25. Quoted in Esslin, *Brecht, The Man and His Work*, p. 84.
26. Hubert Witt, ed., and John Peet, tr., *Brecht As They Knew Him*, p. 201.

images of ruling power, to persuade both elite and mass, either through flattering portraits of ideal worlds (Jacobean Court Masques) or through profound critiques of what must never be (Aristophanes, Brecht), that our world is in part the product of someone's dramatic imagination. To this extent, theatre will always remain a powerful tool for altering the world as we see it, and thereby the world as we experience it.

Bibliography

PART I

Abell, Walter. *The Collective Dream in Art, a Psycho-Historical Theory of Culture Based on Relations Between the Arts, Psychology, and the Social Sciences.* Cambridge, Mass.: Harvard University Press, 1957.

Adkins, A. W. H. *Moral Values and Political Behavior in Ancient Greece.* New York: W. W. Norton & Company, 1972.

Arendt, Hannah. *The Human Condition.* New York: Doubleday Anchor, 1959.

Aries, Philippe. *Western Attitudes Toward Death: From the Middle Ages to the Present.* Translated by Patricia Ranum. Baltimore: Johns Hopkins Press, 1974.

Aristotle. *Constitution of Athens.* Translated by Krut von Fritz and Ernst Kapp. New York: Hafner Publishing Company, 1950.

Artaud, Antonin. *The Theater and Its Double.* Translated by Mary C. Richards. New York: Grove Press, 1958.

Axelos, Kostas. *Héraclite et la philosophie.* Paris: Editions Minuit, 1962.

Baldry, H. C. *The Greek Tragic Theatre.* New York: W. W. Norton and Company, 1971.

Bengtson, Herman, ed. *The Greeks and the Persians, From the Sixth to the Fourth Centuries.* Translated by John Conway. New York: Delacorte Press, 1965.

Bieber, Margarete. *The History of the Greek and Roman Theaters.* Princeton: Princeton University Press, 1961.

Bowra, C. M. *Periclean Athens.* New York: The Dial Press, 1971.

Burke, Kenneth. *A Grammar of Motives.* New York: Prentice-Hall, 1954.

Callahan, Virginia Woods. "Types of Rulers in the Plays of Aeschylus." Ph.D. dissertation, University of Chicago, 1944.

Cornford, Francis. *Thucydides Mythhistoricus.* London: E. Arnold, 1907.

———. *From Religion to Philosophy.* New York: Harper and Row, 1957.

de Coulanges, Fustel. *The Ancient City.* New York: Doubleday Anchor, 1959.

de Romilly, Jacqueline. *Time in Greek Tragedy*. Ithaca: Cornell University Press, 1968.

Dodds, E. R. *The Ancient Concept of Progress*. Oxford: Clarendon Press, 1973.

Dover, K. J. *Greek Popular Morality in the Time of Plato and Aristotle*. Berkeley: University of California Press, 1974.

Ehrenberg, Victor. *Sophocles and Pericles*. Oxford: Basil Blackwell, 1954.

Eliade, Mircea. *The Myth of the Eternal Return, or Cosmos and History*. Translated by Willard R. Trask. New Jersey: Princeton University Press, 1965.

Else, Gerald F. *Aristotle's Poetics: The Argument*. Cambridge, Mass.: Harvard University Press, 1963.

————. *The Origin and Early Form of Greek Tragedy*. New York: The Norton Library, 1972.

Fergusson, Francis. *The Idea of a Theater*. New York: Doubleday Anchor, 1953.

Flickinger, Roy C. *The Greek Theater and Its Drama*. Chicago: University of Chicago Press, 1922.

Frye, Northrop. "The Social Context of Literary Criticism." In *Sociology of Literature and Drama,* Elizabeth and Tom Burns, eds. Baltimore: Penguin Books, 1973.

Glotz, G. *The Greek City and Its Institutions*. New York: A. A. Knopf, 1951.

Grene, David, and Richard Lattimore, eds. *The Complete Greek Tragedies*. Chicago: University of Chicago Press, 1959.

Hall, Edward T. *The Hidden Dimension*. New York: Doubleday and Company, 1966.

Harrison, Jane Ellen. *Themis*. New York: Meridian, 1962.

Harry, Joseph E. *Aeschylus' Prometheus*. London: American Book Company, 1905.

Havelock, E. A. *The Crucifixion of Intellectual Man*. Boston: Beacon Press, 1951.

————. *Preface to Plato*. Cambridge, Mass.: Belknap Press of Harvard University Press, 1963.

Jaeger, Werner. *Paideia: The Ideals of Greek Culture*. Translated by Gilbert Highet. Vol. 1. New York: Oxford University Press, 1945.

Jaspers, Karl. *Tragedy Is Not Enough*. Boston: Beacon Press, 1952.

Kaufmann, Walter. *Tragedy and Philosophy*. New York: Doubleday Anchor, 1969.

Kuhns, Richard. *The House, the City, and the Judge*. New York: Bobbs-Merrill, 1962.

Langer, Suzanne. *Mind: An Essay on Human Feeling*. Vol. I. Baltimore: Johns Hopkins Press, 1967.

Linforth, Ivan M. *Solon the Athenian.* Berkeley: University of California Press, 1919.

Lucas, D. W. *The Greek Tragic Poets.* London: Cohen and West Ltd., 1950.

Lukacs, Georges. "Approximation to Life in the Novel and the Play." In *Sociology of Literature and Drama,* Elizabeth and Tom Burns, eds. Baltimore: Penguin Books, 1973.

Murray, Robert Duff, Jr. *The Motif of Io in Aeschylus' Suppliants.* New Jersey: Princeton University Press, 1958.

Nietzsche, Friedrich. *The Birth of Tragedy.* Translated by Francis Golffing. New York: Doubleday Anchor, 1956.

Paolucci, Anne and Henry, editors. *Hegel on Tragedy.* New York: Doubleday Anchor, 1962.

Pickard-Cambridge, Sir Arthur Wallace. *The Theatre of Dionysus in Athens.* Oxford: The Clarendon Press, 1946.

———. *Dithyramb, Tragedy and Comedy.* Oxford: The Clarendon Press, second edition, 1966.

Pitkin, Hanna. *Wittgenstein and Justice.* Berkeley: University of California Press, 1972.

Plato. *Republic.* Translated by Francis Cornford. Oxford: Oxford University Press, 1960.

———. *The Laws.* Translated by A. E. Taylor. London: J. M. Dent and Sons, 1960.

———. *Theaetetus.* Translated by John McDowell. Oxford: The Clarendon Press, 1973.

Podlecki, Anthony J. *The Political Background of Aeschylean Tragedy.* Ann Arbor: University of Michigan Press, 1966.

Pronko, Leonard C. *Theater East and West. Perspectives Toward a Total Theater.* Berkeley: University of California Press, 1967.

Rank, Otto. *Art and Artist.* Translated by Charles F. Atkinson. New York: A. A. Knopf, 1932.

Rhodes, P. J. *The Athenian Boule.* Oxford: The Clarendon Press, 1972.

Ridgeway, William. *The Early Age of Greece.* Vol. I. Cambridge: Cambridge University Press, 1901.

———. *The Origin of Tragedy, with special reference to the Greek Tragedies.* New York: Benjamin Bloom, Inc., reissued 1966.

Rostovtzeff, M. *The Social and Economic History of the Hellenistic World.* Vol. I. Oxford: Oxford University Press, 1953.

Scharlemann, M. H. "The Influences of the Social Changes in Athens on the Development of Greek Tragedy." Ph.D. dissertation, Washington University, St. Louis, Missouri, 1938.

Sheppard, J. T. *Aeschylus, the Prophet of Greek Freedom.* London: T. Murby and Company, 1943.

Snell, Bruno. *The Discovery of the Mind; The Greek Origins of European Thought.* Translated by T. G. Rosenmeyer. Oxford: Blackwell, 1953.

Stanford, William B. *Aeschylus in His Style: A Study in Language and Personality.* London: Basil Blackwell, 1942.

Stoessl, F. "Aeschylus as a Political Thinker." *American Journal of Philology* (1952), 120-130.

Thucydides. *The Complete Writings of Thucydides. The Peloponnesian War.* Translated by Crawley. Introduction by John H. Finley, Jr. New York: The Modern Library, 1951.

Thompson, George. *Aeschylus, The Prometheus Bound.* Cambridge: Cambridge University Press, 1932.

————. *Aeschylus and Athens: A study in the social origins of Drama.* London: Lawrence and Wishart, 1967.

Wittgenstein, Ludwig. *Philosophical Investigations.* Translated by G. E. M. Anscombe. Oxford: Basil Blackwell, 1958.

Wolin, Sheldon S. *Politics and Vision.* Boston: Little, Brown and Company, 1960.

Yates, Frances. *The Art of Memory.* Chicago: University of Chicago Press, 1974.

PART II

Allen, J. W. *A History of Political Thought in the 16th Century.* London: University Paperbacks, 1960.

Saint Augustine. *City of God.* Translated by Gerald G. Walsh *et al.* New York: Doubleday Anchor, 1958.

Bendix, Reinhard. *Max Weber and Jacob Burckhardt.* Institute of Industrial Relations, No. 257. Berkeley: University of California, 1966.

Bergeron, David M. *English Civic Pageantry, 1558-1642.* London: Edward Arnold Ltd., 1971.

Bradley, A. C. *Shakespearean Tragedy.* New York: Meridian Books, 1961.

Burckhardt, Jacob. *The Civilization of the Rennaissance in Italy.* New York: Phaidon, 1950.

Campbell, Lily B. *Shakespeare's Histories. Mirror of Elizabethan Policy.* San Marino, California: Huntington Library, 1963.

Cavell, Stanley. *Must We Mean What We Say? A Book of Essays.* New York: Scribner and Sons, 1969.

Cochrane, Charles Norris. *Christianity and Classical Culture.* New York: Galaxy Books, 1957.

Danby, John. *Shakespeare's Doctrine of Nature. A Study of King Lear.* London: Faber and Faber, 1949.

Ford, Boris, ed. *The Age of Shakespeare.* Vol. II. London: Cassell, 1961.

Gerth, H. H., and C. Wright Mills. *From Max Weber.* New York: Galaxy Books, 1958.

Grene, David. *Reality and the Heroic Pattern. Last Plays of Ibsen, Shakespeare, and Sophocles.* Chicago: University of Chicago Press, 1967.

Halliday, F. E. *The Life of Shakespeare.* London: Gerald Duckworth and Company, 1961.

Harbage, A. *Shakespeare's Audience.* New York: Columbia University Press, 1961.

Huntington, Samuel. *Political Order in Changing Societies.* New Haven: Yale University Press, 1968.

Jameson, Thomas. *The Hidden Shakespeare. A Study of the Poet's Undercover Activity in the Theater.* New York: Funk and Wagnalls, 1967.

Kernodle, G. *From Art to Theatre. Form and Convention in the Renaissance.* Chicago: University of Chicago Press, 1947.

Knights, L. C. *Drama and Society in the Age of Jonson.* London: Chatto and Windus, 1937.

Kott, Jan. *Shakespeare notre contemporain.* Translated from Polish to French by Anna Posner. Paris: Marabout Université, 1962.

Metzger, Arnold. "Freedom and Death." Translated by Ralph Manheim. *The Human Context,* Vol. IV, No. 1 (1972), 215-242.

Muir, Edwin. *The Politics of King Lear.* Glasgow: Jackson and Company, 1947.

Muir, K. *Last Periods of Shakespeare, Racine and Ibsen.* Detroit: Wayne State University Press, 1961.

Orgel, Stephen. *The Illusion of Power. Political Theater in the English Renaissance.* Berkeley: University of California Press, 1975.

Paolucci, Henry, ed. *The Political Writings of Saint Augustine.* Chicago: Gateway, 1962.

Phillips, James Emerson, Jr. *The State in Shakespeare's Greek and Roman Plays.* New York: Columbia University Press, 1940.

Richmond, H. M. *Shakespeare's Political Plays.* New York: Random House, 1967.

Shakespeare, William. *The Works of William Shakespeare.* New York: Oxford University Press, 1969.

Speaight, Robert. "Shakespeare and Politics." The Royal Society of Literature Lecture, London (May 21, 1946).

Spencer, Theodore. *Shakespeare and the Nature of Man.* New York: Macmillan, 1961.

Steiner, George. *The Death of Tragedy.* New York: A. A. Knopf, 1961.

Thorndike, Ashley H. *Shakespeare's Theater.* New York: Macmillan, 1916.

Tillyard, E. M. W. *The Elizabethan World Picture*. London: Chatto and Windus, 1956.

Whitaker, Virgil K. *The Mirror Up to Nature: The Technique of Shakespeare's Tragedies*. San Marino, California: Huntington Library, 1965.

Wright, Louis B. *Middle-Class Culture in Elizabethan England*. Chapel Hill: University of North Carolina Press, 1935.

Yates, Frances. *Theatre of the World*. Chicago: University of Chicago Press, 1969.

PART III

Althusser, Louis. *For Marx*. Translated by Ben Brewster. New York: Vintage Books. 1970.

Baxandall, Lee. "Brecht in America, 1935." *The Drama Review*, Vol. 12, No. 1 (Fall 1967), 69-87.

Benjamin, Walter. *Understanding Brecht*. Translated by Anna Bostock. London: New Left Books, 1973.

Bentley, Eric, translator. *Seven Plays by Bertolt Brecht*. New York: Grove Press, 1961.

Bottomore, T. B., editor and translator. *Karl Marx, Early Writings*. New York: McGraw-Hill, 1963.

Bowers, Faubian. *Theatre in the East. A Survey of Asian Dance and Drama*. New York: Thomas Nelson and Sons, 1956.

Bradley, A. C. *Oxford Lectures on Poetry*. London: Macmillan, 1923.

Brecht, Bertolt. *Poems on the Theatre*. Translated by John Berger and Anna Bostock. Northwood, Middlesex: Scorpion Press, 1961.

————. *Baal, A Man's A Man, and The Elephant Calf*. Edited by Eric Bentley. New York: Grove Press, 1964.

————. *Edward II. A Chronicle Play*. translated by Eric Bentley. New York: Grove Press, 1966.

————. *Galileo*. Translated by Eric Bentley. New York: Grove Press, 1966.

————. *The Good Woman of Setzuan*. Translated by Eric Bentley. New York: Grove Press, 1966.

————. *Mother Courage*. Translated by Eric Bentley. New York: Grove Press, 1966.

————. "On the Caucasian Chalk Circle." Translated by H. Schmidt and J. Clegg. *The Drama Review*, Vol. 12, No. 1 (Fall 1967), 88-100.

————. *Saint Joan of the Stockyards*. Translated by Frank Jones. Bloomington: Indiana University Press, 1974.

Burke, Kenneth. *Language as Symbolic Action. Essays on Life, Literature and Method*. Berkeley: University of California Press, 1973.

Burns, Elizabeth. *Theatricality. A Study of Convention in the Theatre and in Social Life*. New York: Harper Torchbook, 1973.

Esslin, Martin. *Reflections: Essays on Modern Theatre*. New York: Doubleday and Company, 1969.

————. *Brecht: The Man and His Work*. New York: Doubleday Anchor, 1971.

Ewen, Frederic. *Bertolt Brecht; his life, his art, and his times*. New York: Citadel Press, 1967.

Feuer, Lewis, editor. *Marx and Engels*. New York: Doubleday Anchor, 1959.

Gard, Robert. *Grassroots Theater, A Search for Regional Arts in America*. Madison, Wisconsin: University of Wisconsin Press, 1955.

Gassner, John. *Form and Idea in Modern Theatre*. New York: Dryden Press, 1956.

Geertz, Clifford. *The Interpretation of Cultures. Selected Essays*. New York: Basic Books, 1973.

Guanwardana, A. J. "Theatre in Asia: An Introduction." *The Drama Review*, Vol. 15, No. 2 (Spring 1971), 45-52.

————. "Theatre as a Weapon." *The Drama Review*, Vol. 15, No. 2 (Spring 1971), 226-236.

Hatley, Barbara. "Wayang and Ludruk Polarities in Java." *The Drama Review*, Vol. 15, No. 2 (Spring 1971), 85-95.

Jotterand, Frank. "Theater as an Art-Form is Dying." *Le Monde Weekly* (February 24, 1971), p. 7.

Kott, Jan. "Witkiewicz and the Corpses. On the Dialectic of Anachronism." *Encounter* (February 1970), 60-70.

Landau, Jacob M. *Studies in the Arab Theater and Cinema*. Philadelphia: University of Pennsylvania Press, 1969.

Manheim, R., and J. Willett, translators. *Bertolt Brecht Collected Plays*, Vol. 9. New York: Vintage Books, 1973.

Mannheim, Karl. *Man and Society in an Age of Reconstruction*. New York: Harcourt Brace, 1940.

Mark, Karl. *The 18th Brumaire of Louis Bonaparte*. New York: International Publishers, 1963.

Mark, Karl, and Frederick Engels. *The German Ideology*. Part One. Edited by C. J. Arthur. New York: International Publishers, 1973.

Mészáros, István. *Marx's Theory of Alienation*. New York: Harper Torchbook. 1972.

Mews, Siegfried, editor. *Essays on Brecht: Theatre and Politics*. Chapel Hill: University of North Carolina Press, 1974.

Mills, C. Wright. *The Power Elite*. New York: Oxford Press, 1956.

Mittenzwei, Werner. "Mouvement Perpetuel ou Fin de Partie (Brecht sur les scènes du monde)." *Recherches Internationales,* No. 60 (1969), 5-14.

Nolte, Fred Otto. *The Early Middle-Class Drama (1696-1774).* Lancaster, Pennsylvania: Lancaster Press, 1935.

Peacock, James L. *Rites of Modernization: Symbolic and Social Aspects of Indonesian Proletarian Drama.* Chicago: University of Chicago Press, 1968.

Poggi, Jack. *Theater in America. The Impact of Economic Forces, 1870-1967.* Ithaca, New York: Cornell University Press, 1968.

Spalter, Max. *Brecht's Tradition.* Baltimore: Johns Hopkins Press, 1967.

Suvin, Darko. "The Mirror and the Dynamo. On Brecht's Aesthetic Point of View." *The Drama Review,* Vol. 12, No. 1 (Fall 1967), 62-72.

Tucker, Robert C., editor. *The Marx-Engels Reader.* New York: W. W. Norton and Company, 1972.

Uchiyama Jun. "Doctrine: China, Theatre After 1949." Translated by Kusuhara Tomoko. *The Drama Review,* Vol. 15, No. 2 (Spring 1971), 252-257.

Voegelin, Eric. *From Enlightenment to Revolution.* Edited by John H. Hallowell. Durham, North Carolina: Duke University Press, 1975.

Weber, Max. *Economy and Society,* Vol. III. Edited by Guenther Roth and Claus Wittich. New York: Bedminister Press, 1968.

Weideli, Walter. *The Art of Bertolt Brecht.* Translated by Daniel Russell. New York: New York University Press, 1963.

Wekwerth, Manfred. "From Brecht Today." Translated by Martin Nicolaus. *The Drama Review,* Vol. 12, No. 1 (Fall 1967), 120-130.

Willett, John, editor and translator. *Brecht on Theater.* New York: A Dramabook, 1966.

Witt, Hubert, editor, and John Peet, translator. *Brecht as They Knew Him.* New York: International Publishers, 1974.

Index